GOSPEL HAYMANOT

A Constructive Theology and Critical
Reflection on African and
Diasporic Christianity

GOSPEL HAYMANOT

A Constructive Theology and Critical Reflection on African and Diasporic Christianity

EDITED BY
VINCE L. BANTU

URBAN MINISTRIES, INC.

Copyright © 2020 by Vince Bantu, General Editor

All rights reserved.

No part of this book may be reproduced or transmitted in any form or by any means, electronic or mechanical, including photocopying, recording, video, or by any information or retrieval system, without prior written permission from the publisher except for the use of brief quotations in a book review.

Published in the United States by Urban Ministries, Inc.
P. O. Box 436987
Chicago, IL 60643
www.urbanministries.com

ISBN 978-1-68353-665-9 (paperback)
ISBN 978-1-68353-666-6 (ebook)

Multiple copies of *Gospel Haymanot: A Constructive Theology and Critical Reflection on African and Diasporic Christianity* may be ordered at 1-800-860-8642.

Scripture quotations are taken from the following Bible versions:
New International Version (NIV); New English Translation (NET); New Revised Standard Version (NRSV); The Message (MSG).

Cover design by Laura Duffy
Book design by PearCreative.ca

Printed in the United States of America

For Taína, my noble one

CONTENTS

Foreword (Dr. William E. Pannell)	1
Acknowledgments	5
An Introduction to Gospel Haymanot (Vince L. Bantu)	7
1. FEMINIST, WOMANIST AND GOSPELIST INTERPRETATIONS OF THE DAUGHTERS OF ZELOPHEHAD: Bridging the Gap Amongst Competing Traditions (Quonekuia Day)	57
2. GRACE REVERSED: The Significance and Application of Amos' Reuse of Exodus and Conquest Motifs (Cleotha Robertson)	83
3. WORTHY OF THE GOSPEL: Aliens, Slaves, and Women as Our Teachers (Dennis R. Edwards)	107
4. UNDIVIDED WINGS: Engaging Patristics Through Gospel Haymanot (Vince L. Bantu)	123
5. WORSHIPPING WHILE BLACK: A Peace Studies Analysis of Black Church Origins and the Implications for Gospel Haymanot (Nicholas Rowe)	145
6. HOME COOKING: Evangelical Theology That Includes Us (Vincent Bacote)	169
7. FROM HISTORICAL TRAUMA TO SHALOM (Jacqueline T. Dyer)	181
Conclusion: A Living Haymanot of the Whole Gospel (Vince L. Bantu)	199
Author Biographies	215
Notes	219

FOREWORD

This is an important book. The author represents a growing number of very talented young scholars who are working within the context of both the Black church and the academy. They are taking on the challenge of assisting the Black church in accomplishing its calling. These writers have impeccable credentials from some of the best schools in the land. It is encouraging to this senior as this is taking place at a most crucial of times for the people of God.

This is also an important book because its starting point is the church. Theologians always include the church in their research and writings of course. But they do not usually start there. Dr. Bantu begins there and more so. He knows the old saying among Black believers: "white people go to therapy, Black people go to church." It has long been the case that the church is the most important institution in the black community (it should be in any community, truth be told). Bantu begins this work among ancient Black peoples and brings the peculiar work of the Spirit into the present.

These young scholars know that the Black church is undergoing unprecedented challenges to its significance in the community. For one thing, the old neighborhood has changed. In many urban centers there is no Black neighborhood. From immigration to gentrification, forces combine to push Black people from their homes and businesses. Then there are the challenges posed by newer generations of young Black people for whom the church has not had the attraction shared by grandparents. A professor from a prestigious university argued that the Black church was dead, and for many of his students, especially the Black ones, the church had never been alive. Furthermore, Black pastors are aging, and they are not being replaced by younger people. This was true when C. Eric Lincoln and Lawrence Mamiya wrote their findings in the late 80's.[1] They traced much of this to the success of the civil rights movement. Young Black students found themselves being courted by white colleges and, upon graduation, found opportunities for service much broader than previous generations could imagine. As a result, young people, especially Black males, did not consider the church a viable option. Poor, urban Black working people don't make much of the church either. The feeling seems to be mutual in spite of attempts of some congregations to focus on ministering to the needs of poor people. It's an urban issue and the Black church at its core has never felt comfortable in urban settings. In too many settings it is still an urban church with a rural soul.

Without reasons for hope, there is little need to evangelize, and there is abundant concern within Black leadership that evangelism has gone the way of the dodo. Evangelism is a theological issue and has direct connections with the growth of congregations. It is also crucial to the integrity of the Church whom Jesus charged with the responsibility to go into all the world and make disciples.

This is important reading because of its grounding in theology. Some years ago, white evangelicals engaged in an intramural skirmish some called "the battle for the Bible." Like many exercises among scholars, the outcome made little difference among the folks in the pews. These educators were white and could afford to debate whether the Bible was inerrant in all its ways. In their comfort zones, they knew very little about oppression.

But Black scholars had their own version of the same battle. The core question was whether the Bible was an adequate guide for the liberation of oppressed people. The discussions ranged from North and South America and the Far East. Theologies were developed in shades of black, brown, and red. These were academics and their work eventually trickled down to the seminaries and pulpits of their respective nations. Seeds had been sown which would change traditional ways of defining salvation and the purpose of Jesus in history.

The issues may be different these days, but not much. In fact, they are largely the same, only they are far more universal in scope. As Benjamin Barber put it, "Caught between Babel and Disneyland, the planet is falling precipitously apart and coming reluctantly together at the very same moment." [2]Bantu knows most of this story. Here he is adding his own Gospelist take on it.

Dr. William E. Pannell
Professor Emeritus of Preaching
Fuller Theological Seminary
Pasadena, California
March 25, 2020

ACKNOWLEDGMENTS

As is the case with all good things emerging from African and Diasporic peoples, they are always the collective work of community. This book would not be possible without the love and support of so many throughout our community. The editorial team at Urban Ministries International has gone above and beyond typical publishing support—Jeffrey Wright and Annette Leach, thank you for your belief in this project and support. I am ever grateful for the editorial support of several of my students at Fuller Theological Seminary. I thank my colleagues in this project, whose wisdom and scholarship constitute the central benefit of this book: Cleotha Robertson, Quonekuia Day, Dennis Edwards (whose conversation inspired the book to be written!), Nicholas Rowe, Vincent Bacote, and Jacqueline Dyer—thank you so much for your partnership in this Gospel labor.

There have been so many community and family members that have provided the foundation of this *haymanot*. I thank Greater Life Christian Fellowship of Newark, NJ and Jubilee Community Church of St. Louis, MO for demonstrating to me a Gospel-centered vision of holistic Christian testimony. I thank my mentors who have taught me to walk in the *shalom* of the Jesus Way: Soong-Chan Rah, Terry LeBlanc, Alvin Padilla, and Bil & Paulea Mooney- McCoy. I thank my mother who modelled the Gospel to me as a child; my daughters Taína and Naniki, who are a daily reflection of the Gospel; and to my wife, life-partner and the one whom my heart loves—Diana, for always sanctifying and being sanctified with me through the power of the Gospel.

AN INTRODUCTION TO GOSPEL HAYMANOT

VINCE L. BANTU

"Let my people go, so that they may worship me" (Ex. 8:1). Perhaps the most captivating biblical narrative in the theological imagination of African-American Christians has been the Exodus story of God leading His children Israel from bondage in Egypt to freedom in the Promised Land. Moses went to Pharaoh to proclaim good news for the captive Hebrews; good news of liberation unto covenant relationship with God. Jesus also proclaimed good news—or the Gospel—which heralded freedom, restoration and favor (Lk. 4:18-19). The Gospel means liberation from all forms of oppression and sin through faith in Christ. The Gospel signals freedom through Christ in all areas of life. When the God of Israel sent his servant Moses to declare His message of liberation to Pharaoh, the imperative was followed with a statement of intent: God's desire was freedom for His people *so that* they might worship Him. The foundation of liberation from social oppression is found in the Word of God; the *telos* of social liberation is the worship of God alone. The wholistic and salvific economy of God's Kingdom has been properly embraced and reflected through the theology and life of the African-American church since its inception. Black church communities have for the most part been free from the dualistic binary that has plagued the dominant white church, positing a distinction between the dimensions of spiritual and physical, heavenly and worldly, evangelistic and liberative.

However, while the Black church has stood as a pillar of wholistic theology for four hundred years, what is commonly known as "Black Theology" in the theological academy often does not reflect the biblical perspective of the Black church. While the Liberationist perspective that has characterized much of Black academic theology has helpfully drawn the attention to the problematic white supremacist dualism in much of Western evangelicalism, many Black academic theologians have deviated from biblical views on Scripture, Christology and soteriology with which many of them were raised in the Black church. This present volume seeks to provide constructive reflection on the theology that has already existed in the Black church for four hundred years. The biblical vision of shalom which envisions no distinction between theological orthodoxy and liberative justice for the oppressed—which we call Gospel Haymanot—has been a principal characteristic of African-American Christians since our ethnogenesis.

The name *Gospel Haymanot* is in reference to the living faith tradition of Black descendants of the victims of the Trans-Atlantic Slave Trade which holds firmly to the authority of the divinely inspired Word of God and its call for justice for all of God's creation. The word *gospel* has functioned as a defining aspect of the theological innovation of Blacks in North America and the unique liturgical traditions that have developed in the context of oppression.

Gospel music is rooted in the oral tradition of Negro Spirituals by Black slaves who created songs of lamentation and hope rooted in the Gospel of Jesus Christ.[3] The Scriptures in Romans 1:16 describe the Gospel of Jesus Christ as "the power of God"—indicating God's salvific purpose to empower His people. The aim of this power was "unto salvation," or the Greek word *soterian*, whose lexical cognates can refer to "flourishing," "deliverance," "preservation," and "healing."[4] The words of Scripture reveal the comprehensive and multifaceted nature of God's soteriological economy—the idea of salvation/deliverance being *either* spiritual, physical, *or* social is alien to the thought and world of the Bible. Finally, the power of the Gospel is available to "everyone who believes, to the Jew first and also to the Gentile." This demonstrates that the power of God which is the Gospel is made available to all people, irrespective of ethnic, gender, or economic factors. However, the requirement for inclusion in the People of God is faith—"those who believe." A biblical tenet unpopular with many Black scholars of religion and theology is the requirement of faith in the exclusive lordship of Jesus for salvation. Moreover, it is common among many Black theological scholars to equate the necessity of faith in Christ with white supremacy.[5] However, the necessity of "right belief"—*haymanot rete't* (Ge'ez)—is a concept that Black Christians have embraced as integral to the Gospel throughout the history of Christianity among Africans of the diaspora and the motherland.

In the theological literature of the ancient Ethiopian language called Ge'ez, Black Christian theologians spoke frequently of the importance of "orthodox faith" (*haymanot rete't*). The Ge'ez word *haymanot* can mean "faith," "belief," "religion," "creed," and is a uniquely African-Christian alternative to the dominant, Hellenistic term theology (*theos-* "God"; *logos-* "study" or "discourse").⁶ The word *haymanot* features prominently across ancient Ethiopian theological literature as the concept of "right" or "orthodox" (Geçez: *rete't*) theology was of utmost importance to ancient Christians of the African continent. In a fifteenth-century *dersan*⁷ written by the Ethiopian emperor-theologian Zar'a Ya'qob, the emperor primarily addressed the importance of orthodox *haymanot* ("theology") to be taught in the churches across the Ethiopian Empire and for false teachings to be refuted with the Scriptures. Zar'a Ya'qob highly regarded his Ethiopian people as a people of biblical and orthodox faith. In commenting on how theologians from the Roman Empire would sometimes visit Ethiopia for theological discourse and attempt to impose Romanized Christianity, Zar'a Ya'qob argued fervently for the dignity of indigenous Ethiopian *haymanot*: "The people of Ethiopia are chosen and very good, not in our deeds but in faith (*haymanot*). The faith (*haymanot*) of the people of Ethiopia is as bright as the sun."⁸

One of Zar'a Ya'qob's older contemporaries was also the greatest theologian in the history of the Ethiopian Christian tradition—Giyorgis of Segla. Giyorgis wrote the greatest masterpiece of Ethiopian systematic theology in the early fifteenth century called the *Maṣḥafa Mesṭir* ("Book of the Mystery"). In this book, Giyorgis defends Ethiopian theology against various heretical movements common to the ancient and medieval world (Sabellianism, Arianism, Manicheaism), heretical movements local to Ethiopia (ascribed to a heresiarch named Bitu) as well as dominant European Christianity (Chalcedonian Christology). In response to the attempt at imposing European Chalcedonian theology in Ethiopia, Giyorgis says:

The Patriarch (of Alexandria) with the Egyptian bishops and all their majesties, congratulated the Ethiopians, because God's pleasure was in their Scriptures. Therefore, Isaiah says: 'Egypt will be proud of Ethiopia.' Because the Ethiopians and the Egyptians agree in faith (*haymanot*) and in the priesthood. Then the Romans, together with their Patriarch, their king, their bishops, all the encampments of their communities were covered with shame and humiliation.[9]

Ethiopia also witnessed one of the earliest Christian reform movements in Church history. Over a century before the reforms of Martin Luther in Europe, an Ethiopian monastic figure named Estifanos started a movement that challenged the dominant Ethiopian Church. Among the theological critiques of the dominant church, Estifanos and his followers argued against the involvement of governmental officials in church ordinations, prostrating to the Ethiopian emperor and placing church teaching on the same level of authority with Scripture. Estifanos and his followers were severely persecuted and serve as an inspiration to many Ethiopian Christians today. In his *gadl* ("biography"), it is said about Estifanos that he was a "lamp of Christians" and a "holy pillar of faith (*haymanot*)."[10]

Not only in Ethiopia, but across ancient Christian Africa, the concept of orthodox faith and theology were ardently defended and cultivated. This occurred across the African continent long before the period of European colonial domination and the majority of indigenous African theologies developed in resistance to dominant Roman (and later, European) theology.

Therefore, the idea that the concepts of orthodoxy and heresy are rooted in white supremacy and Western colonialism is without support in African primary sources. African Christians understood that "right faith" (*haymanot rete't*) consisted of biblical teaching and justice for the oppressed. This is something that Black Christians in the diaspora have long understood and articulated through unique liturgical, homiletical, and theological expressions. In the spirit of bringing the lived, wholistic theology of the Black church into the context of theological academia, it is incumbent to resist the urge to continually frame conversations that are theological and academic to nomenclature that is rooted in Greco-Roman and European culture. It is especially important for theologians and Christians of African descent to embrace the African continent that birthed our multicultural network of ancestors. For this reason, we embrace the Ethiopian equivalent for the common Western term "theology": *haymanot*. And it is to the *haymanot* of African diasporic communities and the role the Gospel has played in shaping this *haymanot* that this discourse now turns.

An Incomplete Gospel

The majority of Christian theological discourse has been split into two halves—the result of what has been called the Fundamentalist-Modernist Controversy. Beginning in the mid-nineteenth century, European biblical scholars influenced by the Enlightenment began to doubt the authority and historicity of Scripture. As this debate moved across the Atlantic, it was encapsulated in the summer of 1922 when Harry Emerson Fosdick preached the famous sermon "Shall the Fundamentalists Win?" and Clarence Macartney preached the counter-sermon two months later called "Shall Unbelief Win?" The group known by their detractors as "Modernists" began to question the "Fundamentalist" beliefs regarding the authority and historical reliability of the claims of Scripture, the existence of miracles and the exclusive truth of the Gospel.[11] The heightened emphasis on theological orthodoxy among conservative Christian "Fundamentalists" led to two problematic theological trends still prominent in Western evangelicalism: 1.) a subordination of social justice to theological orthodoxy and 2.) an inconsistent public faith that selectively engages political issues while failing to address matters of systemic injustice. The first of these evangelical deviations was encapsulated by Dwight Moody who saw the world as a "wrecked ship" and the Gospel as being first a message of spiritual salvation, with social justice being secondary:

> When I was at work for the City Relief Society, before the fire, I used to go to a poor sinner with the Bible in one hand and a loaf of bread in the other…My idea was that I could open a poor man's heart by giving him a load of wood or a ton of coal when the winter as coming on, but I soon found out that he wasn't any more interested in the Gospel on that account. Instead of thinking how he could come to Christ, he was thinking how long it would be before he got the load of wood. If I had the Bible in one hand and a loaf in the other the people always looked first at the loaf; and that was just the contrary of the order laid down in the Gospel.[12]

The white evangelical imagination which proffers selective political engagement around certain issues while ignoring matters of systemic injustice was exemplified in Billy Graham's acceptance of Jim Crow segregation as a "social" rather than "biblical" issue:

"We follow the existing social customs in whatever part of the country in which we minister. As far as I have been able to find in study of the Bible, it has nothing to say about segregation or nonsegregation. I came to Jackson only to preach the Bible and not to enter into local issues."[13]

Advancing the early theological tenents of the Social Gospel, white liberal Christians went to the other extreme and elevated the social and political aspects of the Gospel while denying the necessity of theological orthodoxy. Influenced by the Social Gospel, the mid- and late twentieth century witnessed the advent of various forms of Liberation Theology drawing attention to the Gospel implications on liberation for the oppressed and disregarding the exclusive truth of the Gospel. The core aspect of what has gotten lost in much of Black academic theology and new religious movements is the reality that God's desire for our liberation is *so that* we may worship Christ alone.

In his influential ethnographic study *Black Gods of the Metropolis*, anthropologist Arthur Fauset examines African-American religious cults that emerged in the urban North during the early twentieth century. Such religious groups, however, do not account for a significant proportion of the African-American community.[14] One of the commonalities of these new religious movements—predominately variations of Christianity, Islam, and Judaism—is that their founders and adherents have a background in Christianity. Fauset lists "dissatisfaction with Christianity" right under "racial or nationalist urge" in a list of the primary motivating factors leading African-Americans into these movements.[15]

The thesis advanced here is that idolatrous pursuit and attainment of heightened levels of social and economic autonomy have led to heretical religious movements and theological trajectories in the African-American religious community and scholarship. The commonality between both heretical Black religious movements and theological scholarship is their tendency to place Black identity and autonomy at the center of religious life. Contemporary African-American religious scholarship tends to prioritize the life and experience of Black people over God in religious activity, thus "displacing the romantic racialist view that cast blacks primarily as the worldly agents of Christ's redemption."[16] However, a theological imagination that centers the human experience in reference to the atoning work of Jesus is neither a "romantic" or a "racialist" view but the fulfillment of the God of Israel who proclaimed to His people that "I have redeemed you; I have called you by name, you are mine" (Is. 43:1). The Word of God implores His people that we are "God's special possession, that you may declare the praises of him who called you out of darkness into his wonderful light" (1 Pt. 2:9). Indeed, Christians from every ethnic group are "agents of Christ's redemption" and our ultimate purpose in life is to glorify the risen Jesus.

The liberation of the oppressed is an important component of how God chooses to glorify Himself among His creation. It has been a human tendency throughout the totality of history to prioritize God's creation over the person of God; this applies to God's activity. In the case of Black liberation, this crucial aspect of the Gospel has been elevated to a problematic

level. This tendency is clear in the seminal text on Black Christian Nationalism, the theological system of the Pan-African Orthodox Christian Church: "Believing that nothing is more sacred than the liberation of Black people, we are a revolutionary Pan-African movement dedicated to the building of a heaven on earth in the here and now for all Black people everywhere."[17] It is of note that the Black church has been the central organization for African-Americans for the whole of our history, that this church has been predominately orthodox and that the Black church developed principally in the South. It is of note that many of the Black new religious movements, mainline liberal Christian churches and liberal Black theology—all who share the commonality of supplanting the centrality of Jesus with Blackness—all emerged primarily in the urban North. Sociologist Edward Franklin Frazier describes the decline of the influence of the Black church during the Great Migration thusly:

> It was inevitable that the Negro should be drawn into the organized forms of social life in the urban environment. As a consequence, the Negro church has lost much of its influence as an agency of social control. Its supervision over the marital and family life of Negroes has declined. The church has ceased to be the chief means of economic cooperation. New avenues have been opened to all kinds of business ventures in which secular ends and values are dominant. The church is no longer the main arena for political active which was the case when Negroes were disfranchised in the South…We have seen how lower-class Negroes have reacted to the cold impersonal environment of the city and of the large denominational churches by joining the 'storefront' churches and the various cults. These all represented their reaction to the crumbling traditional organization of Negro life as Negroes are increasingly cast afloat in the mainstream of American life where they are still outsiders.[18]

It was in the context of the urban migration throughout the mid-twentieth century that the Black church lost much of its orthodox influence in the lives of many Blacks, leaving them open to a myriad of problematic theological movements. In the early twenty-first century, Black theology is broadly accepted as synonymous with the liberationist perspective developed by James Cone. The religious trend in some African-American communities that supplanted the centrality of Christ in religious discourse found a voice in the academy with Cone's seminal text *Black Theology and Black Power*. In this opening manifesto, Cone outlines one of the central tenants of liberation theology—God's preferential option for the poor: "In Christ, God enters human affairs and takes sides with the oppressed."[19] Cone expands on this concept and brilliantly critiques the "theological bankruptcy" of much of white, Western theology: "What has the gospel to do with the oppressed of the land and their struggle for liberation? Any theologian who fails to place that question at the center of his work has ignored the essence of the gospel."[20] Cone's theological method finds echoes in the founder of Liberation Theology, Gustavo Gutiérrez—who helpfully demonstrates the futility of "spiritual/corporeal" binaries in much of Western theology: "Salvation is not something otherworldly, in regard to which the present life is merely a test.

Salvation—the communion of human beings with God and among themselves—is something which embraces all human reality, transforms it, and lead it to its fullness in Christ."[21]

As liberation theology reached the U.S.—predominately in the urban North like many of the religious movements studied by Fauset—symbols of Black oppression found empowering resonance in the story of Scripture. One such prominent example is the typological correlation drawn by Cone in his

The Cross and the Lynching Tree: "In that era, the lynching tree joined the cross as the most emotionally charged symbols in the African American community—symbols that represented both death and the promise of redemption, judgment and the offer of mercy, suffering and the power of hope."[22] Another prominent example of liberationist typology serves as the foundation for Womanist theology—that is, the theological reflection emerging from the perspective of Black women. A colleague of Cone at Union Seminary, Delores Williams penned the foundational Womanist text *Sisters in the Wilderness* and draws heavily from the Hagar narrative in Genesis 16 as a point of departure for Womanist god-talk:

> Hagar's heritage was African as was black women's. Hagar was a slave. Black American women had emerged from a slave heritage and still lived in light of it. Hagar was brutalized by her slave owner, the Hebrew woman Sarah. The slave narratives of African-American women and some of the narratives of contemporary day-workers tell of the brutal or cruel treatment black women have received from the wives of slave masters and from contemporary white female employers. Hagar had no control over her body. It belonged to the slave owner, whose husband, Abraham, ravished Hagar. A child Ishmael was born, mother and child were eventually cast out of Abraham's and Sarah's home without resources for survival. The bodies of African-American slave women were owned by their masters. Time after time they were raped by their owners and bore children whom the masters seldom claimed—children who were slaves—children and their mothers

who slave-master fathers often cast out by selling them to other slave holders. Hagar resisted the brutalities of slavery by running away. Black American women have a long resistance history that included running away from slavery in the antebellum era. Like Hagar and her child Ishmael, African- American female slaves and their children, after slavery, were expelled from the homes of many slave holders and given no resources for survival. Hagar, like many women throughout African-American women's history, was a single parent. But she had serious personal and salvific encounters with God—encounters which aided Hagar in the survival struggle of herself and her son. Over and over again, black women in the churches have testified about their serious personal and salvific encounters with God, encounters that helped them and their families survive.[23]

There is much in liberation theology to be celebrated. Beginning with Gutiérrez, liberationists provided a needed check to the dominant Western theological perspective that implicated Christian discourse with a dualistic worldview that divorced Christian public witness from social liberation: "Sin is not only an impediment to salvation in the afterlife. Insofar as it constitutes a break with God, sin is a historical reality, it is a breach of the communion of persons with each other…And because sin is a personal and social intrahistorical reality, a part of the daily events of human life, it is also, and above all, an obstacle to life's reaching the fullness we call salvation."[24] The liberationist perspective has provided several magnificent correctives for white hegemonic theology and the pacified theology of the

Black church. Cone's critique of American theological academia is adept and accurate:

> Few American theologians have made that identification with the poor blacks in America but have themselves contributed to the system which enslaves black people. The seminaries in America are probably the most obvious sign of the irrelevance of theology to life. Their initiative in responding to the crisis of black people in America is virtually unnoticeable. Their curriculum generally is designed for young white men and women who are preparing to serve all-white churches.[25]

Liberationist perspectives have been a helpful corrective for the dominant white theological dualism and should not be reduced to "Marxist victimology."[26] Cone understands much of the Black church of his contemporary 1960s to have departed from much of its liberative scope of the eighteenth and nineteenth centuries: "The black church, though spatially located in the community of the oppressed, has not responded to the needs of its people."[27] Cone quotes from the document "Black Power: Statement by National Committee of Negro Churchmen," which was a joint statement by various Black, mainline New England pastors calling for prophetic reform in the Black church to support efforts for Black power:

> Too often the Negro church has stirred its members away from the reign of God in this world to a distorted and complacent view of an otherworldly conception of God's power. We commit ourselves as churchmen to make more meaningful in the life of our institution

our conviction that Jesus Christ reigns in the "here" and "now" as well as in the future he brings in upon us. We shall, therefore, use more of the resources of our churches in working for human justice in the places of social change and upheaval where our Master is already at work.[28]

Despite the helpful correctives Black liberation theology has provided, it has ultimately created a gospel message that is equally incomplete as that of white evangelicalism. The centrality of the Black experience for liberation theology is advanced by Cone who advocates "a systematic and comprehensive exposition of the Christ faith using the black experience of struggle as the chief source."[29] The centrality of the Black experience, a cornerstone of Black heretical religious and theological perspectives emerging in the middle-twentieth century, leads to unbiblical universalistic discourse in Cone: "I still regard Jesus Christ today as the chief focus of my perspective on God but not to the exclusion of other religious perspectives. God's reality is not bound by one manifestation of the divine in Jesus but can be found wherever people are being empowered to fight for freedom. Life-giving power or the poor and the oppressed is the *primary criterion* that we must use to judge the adequacy of our theology, not abstract concepts [emphasis added]."[30]

Following Gutiérrez, Cone has reversed the unbiblical dichotomy prioritizing the spiritual over the social inherent to white, Western evangelical theology and created a liberationist dichotomy that subjugates theological orthodoxy to social action. Gutiérrez likewise states that "persons are saved if they open themselves up to God and to others, even if they are not clearly aware that they are doing so" and that "they reject God insofar as they turn away from the building up of this world, do not open themselves to others, and culpably withdraw into themselves."[31] For liberationists, social justice is the primary criteria for salvation and theological orthodoxy is either subordinated or cast aside as an irrelevant exercise in social oppression. In the same way, Womanist theology celebrates and calls for the "business of accommodating the Bible to life,"[32] which often includes "an internal critique of the Bible."[33]

The result of this fabricated division in the biblical Gospel has been theological institutions that emphasize either biblical orthodoxy or social justice. In the worst case, opposing sides will defend one of these and outright deny the validity of the other; in the best case, both will be acknowledged as important, but one will be prioritized over the other. The important point for the present discussion is that these various theological camps have been invented by white people. The Black church, wrought with unimaginable oppression and undergirded by the power of the Gospel of Jesus Christ, has always understood the inseparable nature of biblical truth and justice. However, much of Black academic theology has imbibed the white liberal theological perspective, often for two reasons: 1.) understandable reaction against the idols of white supremacy, materialistic triumphalism and American exceptionalism in evangelical theology and 2.) an increased amount of solidarity and support from white liberal denominations and theological institutions. The resultant situation is a theological landscape dominated by a fragmented white theological binary with a small presence of Black theologians largely espousing a white liberal paradigm that does not reflect the belief of the majority of the Black church. The purpose of this present volume is to provide constructive theological reflection from scholars embracing the wholistic

Gospel Haymanot of the Black church which holds firmly to the exclusive truth of the Gospel of Jesus Christ and disrupts systems of injustice for the empowerment of the oppressed.

A Gospelist Reading of Scripture

The word "gospel" has been at the core of the African-American Christian experience from the start. Gospel music, "the very fruit of the African-American church,"[34] is an art form that is inherently Christian and African that calls for freedom as confidently as it stands on the authority of Scripture. Gospel music flows through the veins of the Black Christian experience and expresses the core of this biblical concept—"good news." Just as the word "Gospel" stands at the heart of the Black Christian experience, the Gospel of Jesus Christ is the core of God's self-revelation in Scripture. The Gospel of Mark, widely taken to be the earliest of the four gospels, opens by declaring the *euangelion* ("good news," "Gospel") of Jesus Christ. The Gospel is variably referred to as the "Gospel of God" (Mk. 1:14; Rom. 15:16), "the Gospel of Jesus Christ," (Mk. 1:1; 1 Cor. 9:12), "the Gospel of the Kingdom," (Mt. 4:23; 9:35; 24:14), "the Gospel of the grace of God," (Acts 20:24), "the Gospel of the glory of Christ," (2 Cor. 4:4), "the gospel of peace" (Eph. 6:15), and "an eternal Gospel" (Rev. 14:6).

The Gospel belongs to the triune God. The ultimate aim of the Gospel is to administer the grace of God for the glory of God. God is the beginning and the end of the Gospel. Theological discourse must begin and end with God.[35] The "good news" proclaimed in Scripture and encapsulated in the life, death and resurrection of Jesus Christ is intricately tied to the Kingdom of God. The reign of God, fully realized in the resurrection of Christ, reigns in heaven and on earth (Mt. 6:10). The "good news" of the Kingdom means that God is fully in control of everything and that humanity can participate in the Kingdom through the forgiveness of sins. Sin is personal and corporate (Ps 106:6; Is. 6:5; Jer. 3:25; Acts 7:51). God holds individuals and nations accountable for the transgression of His holy standards. The chief characteristic of God's Kingdom is that of *shalom*, the setting right of all things—personal and corporate.

The biblical concept of *shalom* perfectly illustrates God's desire for right belief and right action to exist interdependently. The purpose of God's work in the world through Israel was to bring *shalom* to all creation. The Hebrew concept of *shalom* is often translated as "peace." However, this word means so much more. *Shalom* does not mean "peace" in the sense that is often meant as an absence of conflict. Rather, biblical *shalom* is the presence of justice, wholeness and all things being made right. The *shalom*-oriented purview of the Kingdom of God envisions the reconciliation between God and creation. The vertical unity between God and humanity which Christ paid for on the cross is inseparable from the horizontal unity that brings *shalom* between people groups. Just as true religion does not exist without being accompanied by justice (Jas. 1:27), liberation for the oppressed is without purpose apart from being made alive by grace through faith in Christ (Eph. 2:8-9). When Jesus quotes the prophet Isaiah in the temple at the beginning of his public ministry, he affirmed that the "good news" that He was sent to proclaim held a special priority for the poor, oppressed, sick, and imprisoned (Lk. 4:18-19).

The language of Scripture is a further clue into the wholistic nature of the Gospel. In the English language, the words "righteousness" and "justice" have very different connotations.

The concept of righteousness tends to evoke personal piety and inner-moral rectitude while justice evokes a more corporate, social level of fairness and equality. The beauty of the world of Scripture is that these concepts are all encapsulated in the Greek word *dikaiosune*. The word *dikaiosune* can be translated as either "righteousness" or "justice" depending on the context as this concept can apply to personal, moral integrity and social justice. However, many modern Bible translations, influenced by Western dualistic theology, will often over-translate *dikaiosune* as "righteousness," when it may be more appropriate to use "justice." For example, when Jesus said "Blessed are those who are persecuted for the sake of *dikaiosune*, for theirs is the Kingdom of Heaven" (Mt. 5:10), most Western Bible translations use "righteousness" here.[36] However, it is much less likely that the first-century Palestinian Jewish context to which Jesus spoke would have been persecuted for the sake of Torah observance. Rather, persecution for the sake of social and economic injustice would have been the more likely reason one would experience persecution.

A Gospelist reading of Scripture is informed by the interdependent relationship between truth and justice. Gospel Haymanot holds firmly to the biblical priorities of orthodoxy and social action without prioritizing one over the other; moreover, Gospel Haymanot rejects any alleged distinction between the two. John cautions believers that "if anyone has material possessions and sees a brother or sister in need but has no pity on them, how can the love of God be in that person?" (1 Jn. 3:17). Peter and John declared before the Sanhedrin their commitment to fulfilling God's commands, even to the point of civil disobedience (Acts 4:19). God's commands are further clarified by the prophet Micah: "And what does the Lord require of you? To act justly and to love mercy and to walk humbly with God" (Mic. 6:8). The prophet Isaiah declared that prayers and fasting unaccompanied with justice remain unheard and unanswered by God (Is.58:1-5). In his opening oracle, Isaiah declared to Israel that God hid His eyes from their worship and hid His ears from their prayers because of their oppression of the marginalized (Is. 1:15).

This same passage provided voice for African-American Christians such as Frederick Douglass who frequently interpreted white Americans' celebration of the Fourth of July through the lens of this Isaiah passage.[37]

The centrality of God's justice in the manifestation of His Kingdom problematizes a theological system that protects the sensitivities of the privileged and incriminates the poor, the prisoner, and the sojourner. Even a cursory reading of Scripture makes plain God's focused concern for the poor and His expectation that His people are actively involved in ending suffering and oppression. When the most marginalized of society—the poor, widows, and orphans—are mentioned in Scripture, one finds imperatives to empower and care for such people rather than blaming them for their own poverty (Deut. 15:7-8; Prov. 22:22-23; Jer. 22:3; Rom.12:13). Passages dealing with immigrants and refugees are not accompanied with statements of mistrust towards these groups or concern for the national security and financial vitality of the hosts; rather one finds commands to welcome openly and care for the sojourner (Lev. 19:33-34; Deut. 27:19; Jer. 7:5-7; Ez. 47:22; Zech. 7:9-10; Matt. 25:35; Heb. 13:2). Scripture referencing slavery and prisoners are both accompanied with imperatives to care for and liberate such groups—not to punish or ostracize them (Ex.

21:16; Deut. 23:15-16; Ps. 69:33; 102:20; Is. 61:1; Matt. 25:36; Col. 4:1; Phil. 1:16; Heb. 13:3).

The same Gospel that empowered African-American Christians to fight for freedom from slavery is now crying out for justice from a racist and unjust policing and incarceration system that disproportionately penalizes people of color for financial profit in ways very similar to slavery and Jim Crow segregation.[38] Gospel Haymanot unapologetically condemns the systemic sins of injustice and calls for God's people in all times and places to be beacons of justice in the world. Much of Western evangelical theology prioritizes spiritual salvation and sees social justice as an elective. Even when issues of justice are addressed, there is an unbalanced support of poverty aid initiatives while ignoring efforts of addressing the causes of oppression. This is not to disparage the indispensable work of mercy ministry, immediate aid, and community development. Rather, the issue here is white evangelicalism's inconsistent public faith that ignores challenging systems of power in matters affecting the most oppressed of society.

Because engaging in social justice is subordinated to the "spiritual" disciplines of evangelism and discipleship, the idols of white supremacy, male patriarchy, syncretistic nationalism, and classism are tolerated in much of white evangelicalism. Personal sins relating to personal purity and piety are addressed sternly, but when systemic injustice manifests in the Church, there is greater lenience extended in hopes that believers grasp God's heart for justice. The Church must treat the sin of systemic injustice as seriously as we treat personal sins of impiety or theological heresy. An inverted biblical exegesis that criminalizes the poor and the immigrant and venerates the nations and social classes of power is just as theologically problematic as claiming that Jesus is not the Son of God or that He did not rise from the grave (Mt. 25:40). This does not preclude the need for grace in how we engage in discipleship nor the humility that comes in realizing our corporate complicity in injustice. However, this is a call to take more seriously the role of justice in the life of following Jesus.

When Jesus calls the privileged to follow Him in ways that will cost wealth and reputation, He does not modify or apologize for these radical requirements. Gospel Haymanot embraces the call of pursuing liberation for the oppressed and its inseparableness from orthodox theology. Gospel Haymanot arises from a Black experience that cannot treat injustice as an optional aspect of the life of faith: "Black faith was forged in the midst of the perverse and tragic paradoxes of black life. It is a faith, therefore, that does not ignore the unthinkable and irrational terror of black living. It takes it seriously…Indeed, the faith born in slavery provided a weapon to resist and to fight against the religiously legitimated tyranny of America's Anglo-Saxon exceptionalism."[39]

Likewise, theology that places the liberation of the oppressed as an end in and of itself is unbiblical and theologically bankrupt. When Jesus rebuked the self-righteousness of the Pharisees who desired to stone an adulterous woman, He also told the woman, "Go, and sin no more" (Jn. 8:11). As Carl Ellis has stated: "the oppressed *must* fight to break the back of oppression so they can seek God's solution to their *own* unrighteousness."[40] This perspective was mirrored by J. Deotis Roberts who issued a challenge to the Liberationist perspective at its beginning: "Sin as self-centeredness is a disease that inflicts the black community as well as the white community."[41] Gospel Haymanot calls the oppressed to be sanctified from their own sin and partners with privileged allies desirous to participate in the beloved community.

Zacchaeus was a tax collector who decided to follow Jesus and provide reparations for those he cheated.

Despite protests of the watching crowd, Jesus embraced Zacchaeus and declared this former tax collector a recipient of God's salvation (Lk. 19:9).

People of privilege should neither despise nor abuse their social standing; rather, the Gospel calls those in power to leverage social capital for the justice of God's Kingdom. The call of Jesus on all to follow Him is an exclusive one. Jesus said, "I am the way and the truth and the life. No one comes to the Father except through me" (Jn. 14:6). The apostles declared that "Salvation is found in no one else, for there is no other name under heaven given to mankind by which we must be saved" (Acts 4:12). Gospel Haymanot takes the entire Bible as authoritative and rejects dualistic tendencies of selectively embracing and rejecting various components of Scripture. Embracing the orthodoxy of the Gospel while neglecting its call to justice is equally as problematic as highlighting the liberative aspects of Scripture while ignoring its claim to absolute and exclusive truth. A Gospelist reading of Scripture is evident in the powerful faith of African-American theologians throughout history.

Gospel Haymanot in Black Christian Tradition

The wholistic nature of the Gospel has shaped African-American spirituality from the beginning. Of the millions of Africans trafficked to the Western Hemisphere through the Trans-Atlantic Slave Trade, few of them were Christians prior to their enslavement.[42] In the early years of the American colonies, white missionaries convinced many slave owners to share the Gospel with slaves and argued that Christianity would make Africans into better slaves.[43] Despite this early white supremacist vision of "Christian Slavery," African Christians received the true Gospel which empowered them to express liberation through worship. Negro spirituals serve as some of the earliest windows into African-American Christian theology and are a masterful example of contextualized theological expression that is simultaneously Christian and African. Spirituals served as hermeneutical expressions of freedom rooted in Holy Scripture:

> Oh, you got Jesus, hold him fast
> One more river to cross
> Oh, better love was never told
> One more river to cross
> 'Tis sweeter than honeycomb
> One more river to cross
> One more river to cross
> I pray, good Lord, shall I be one?
> One more river to cross

Liberation from oppression was constantly expressed in language emerging from the Exodus narrative and is inextricable from "holding fast" to the Gospel of Christ. The "crossing of the Jordan" into the Promised Land expressed the biblical imperative for justice on the part of the oppressed:

> No more auction block for me
> No more, no more
> No more auction block for me
> Many thousand gone

Negro spirituals best represent the comprehensive theological vision that held together the universal truth of the Gospel and its call for justice and liberation for the oppressed. These theologically rich, poetic compositions simultaneously expressed hope in the risen Savior and provided strategy for escaping to freedom. The statement is true that "the American Negro church represents the one institution among Negroes in the United States where we are privileged to observe the seeds of revolt."[44] This reality is illustrated in the Stono Rebellion of 1739 in the British-ruled South Carolina colony. This was the largest African revolt in the British colonies of what would become the United States claiming approximately 25 white and 40 Black lives. The African slaves—led by an individual named in white documentation as Jemmy—were attempting to escape to Spanish-controlled Florida in response to the Spanish Empire's promise of freedom for any slave who escapes British colonies. Perhaps the most fascinating aspect of this slave rebellion is that the revolutionists were slaves from the Kingdom of Kongo and were already Christians. The following account attests to the Kongolese Christian ancestry of these freedom fighters:

> Amongst the Negroe Slaves there are a people brought from the Kingdom of Angola in Africa, many of these speak Portugueze (which Language is as near Spanish as Scotch is to English,) by reason that the Portugueze have considerable Settlement, and the Jesuits have a Mission and School in that Kingdom and many Thousands of the Negroes there profess the Roman Catholic Religion.[45]

For many of the African Christians of the Stono Rebellion, it was the Gospel's liberative nature that inspired them to take up arms to fight for liberty. The account continues: "Several Negroes joined them, they calling out Liberty, marched on with Colours displayed, and two Drums beating."[46] This contemporary account attests to one hundred African slaves in South Carolina joining the insurrection which eventually fell to white militia farmers. What is significant is that one of the largest African insurrections in United States history was led by Kongolese slaves whose kingdom had independently adopted Christianity three hundred years prior. For these revolutionists, the Gospel meant that they were made free and were not subject to the rule of earthly oppressors. The Gospel has been the single greatest motivation for Black liberation in African and Diasporic history.

It must also be remembered that oppressive, Eurocentric Christianity was not the first introduction to the Bible for all Black Christians. Ethiopia has been a predominately Christian nation since the fourth century with its own unique theological, liturgical and cultural expression of *haymanot*. By the time Europeans began colonizing the planet while defaming the name of Jesus, Ethiopians had already been a Christian nation for over a thousand years. The Portuguese arrived in Ethiopia in the early seventeenth-century and capitalized on Christian-Islamic wars in East Africa to build an alliance with the Ethiopian *Negus* ("king") Susenyos. However, this alliance entailed *Negus* Susenyos' embracing European Catholicism and rejecting the ancient, indigenous tradition of Ethiopia. This top-down embrace of European Christianity was widely rejected by the Ethiopian people and was ultimately reversed by Susenyos' son Fasilides. One of the principle leaders of this anti-colonial movement was a monastic leader named Walatta Petros ("daughter of Peter").

Walatta Petros resisted her husband—an imperial official— the *Negus* Susenyos and the European colonists as she galvanized the nation to embrace their indigenous Ethiopian traditions and reject European Christianity. Walatta Petros' biography says that "*Negus* Susinyos began to make changes and established the filthy faith of the Europeans" and that when Walatta

Petros was brought before the king she boldly declared that "I am confident, however, that nothing can make me abandon the love for God through Jesus Christ."[47] The Europeans were attempting to impose a Chalcedonian, two-nature Christology, which the Ethiopians had rejected for over a thousand years since the Council of Chalcedon in 451 CE. For Walatta Petros, the doctrine of the essential oneness (*tawahido*) of Jesus' nature—both human and divine—was an essential foundation of *haymanot ret'et* ("orthodox theology") for which she was willing to die. This makes any claim that Black theology is unconcerned with "abstract" principles about God and only concerned with matters of social liberation untenable. For Walatta Petros—a Black, African, lesbian, monastic leader, and revolutionary—resisting European colonialism and heresy were one and the same task. Walatta Petros, one of the principal female saints of the Ethiopian Church to this day, boldly stood upon the Bible as the Word of God as she defended a *ret'et* understanding of sexuality, Christology, the Bible and African liberation.

As Africans migrated across the Motherland and eventually found themselves victims of the Middle Passage, the same engrained pursuit of liberation persisted as it found new Christocentric expression on the other side of the Atlantic. The pursuit of liberation for Black Christians was rooted in the unwavering belief in a historical risen Christ. Jesus was not an idea or an option but represented the absolute truth. These socially coded, liturgical compositions beckoned all hearers to repent from sin and pledge exclusive allegiance to the Lord Jesus Christ:

> Sinner, please don't let this harvest pass
> Sinner, please don't let this harvest pass

> Sinner, please don't let this harvest pass
> And die and lose your soul at last
> Sinner, O see the cruel tree
> Sinner, O see the cruel tree
> Sinner, O see the cruel tree
> Where Christ died for you and me
> My God is a mighty man of war
> My God is a mighty man of war
> My God is a mighty man of war
> Sinner, please don't let this harvest pass

The missionary impulse of Scripture is echoed here imploring fallen humans to hastily come to the throne of grace to receive salvation from God's wrath through Christ's atonement. In the same way, the Apostle Peter exhorted the crowd at the Jerusalem Temple: "Repent, then and turn to God, so that your sins may be wiped out, that times of refreshing may come from the Lord" (Acts 3:19). The next day, Peter and John told the Sanhedrin that "salvation is found in no one else, for there is no other name under heaven given to mankind by which we must be saved" (Acts 4:12). Black slaves understood the exclusive offer of salvation made available only through Christ and the necessity of faith in Him:

> Ride on King Jesus!
> No man can hinder him
> Ride on King Jesus!
> No man can hinder him
> If you want to find your way to God
> No man can hinder him
> The gospel highway must be trod
> No man can hinder him

The urgency of salvation from social oppression was as urgent for slaves as salvation from the eternal punishment of sin and death:

> You better get a home in that rock
> Don't you see
> You better get a home in that rock
> Don't you see
> Between the earth and sky
> I can hear my Savior cry
> You better get a home in that rock
> Oh, don't you see

Black Gospel Haymanot is a *haymanot* ("faith") that is concerned with orthodoxy and orthopraxy. There is perhaps no greater example of solid faith in Christ amidst unspeakable persecution than that of Black women who have continued to endure marginalization from Black males in addition to bearing the weight of Black oppression in America. Despite the fact that Black women have continuously formed the "backbone" of the Black church, they have all too often been kept in the "background." Yet despite the double-oppression of being Black and woman, countless Black Christian female leaders and theologians have been empowered by the Gospel to fight for freedom.[48]

One of the earliest examples of theological work produced by an African-American female was that of Phillis Wheatley. Born circa 1753 somewhere in West Africa, Phillis Wheatley was taken as a slave to Boston on the ship *The Phillis* in her early childhood. Phillis was purchased by the Wheatley family and was given a classical education. Wheatley was the first African-American female poet to be published and her works drew the attention of figures such as George Washington, King George III, and Voltaire. Wheatley converted to Christianity upon hearing the preaching of the revivalist George Whitefield during the first Great Awakening. Much of her writing reflects on slavery and the American construct of Blackness through an African-American Christian theological perspective. Perhaps the most famous such example is her renowned poem *On Being Brought from Africa to America*:

> 'Twas mercy brought me from my Pagan land,
> Taught my benighted soul to understand
> That there's a God, that there's a Saviour too:
> Once I redemption neither sought nor knew.
> Some view our sable race with scornful eye,
> "Their colour is a diabolic die."
> Remember, Christians, Negros, black as Cain,
> May be refin'd, and join th' angelic train.[49]

Despite Wheatley's appellation of "pagan" in reference to Africa, the frequent emphasis on the role and effects of the sun across her literary corpus has been commonly understood to be a feature of her indigenous African religious upbringing.[50] Wheatley's vision of the peculiar institution of slavery was complex and not reducible only to a soteriological mechanism of divine providence. Wheatley denounced slavery in a public address to William Legge 2nd, Earl of Dartmouth who presided as British secretary of state over the North American colonies:

> No more, America, in mournful strain
> Of wrongs, and grievance uredress'd complain
> No longer shall thou dread the iron chain,
> Which wanton Tyranny with lawless hand

Had made, and with it meant t'enslave the land.
Should you, my lord, while you peruse my song,
Wonder from whence my love of Freedom sprung,
Whence flow these wishes for the common good,
By feelings hearts alone best understood,
I, young in life, by seeming cruel fate
Was snatch'd from Afric's fancy'd happy feat:
What pangs excruciating must molest,
What sorrows labour in my parent's breast?
Steel'd was that soul and by no misery mov'd
That from a father seiz'd his babe belov'd:
Such, such my case. And can I then but pray
Others may never feel tyrannic sway?[51]

Wheatley's commitment to biblical orthodoxy did not preclude such public denouncements of the evils of slavery. A contemporary exposition on the Gospel was from the autobiography of Olaudah Equiano in *The Interesting Narrative of the Life of Olaudah Equiano*, published in 1789. In his account, Equiano describes his abduction from his native Nigeria to slavery in South Carolina at the age of eleven. Raised a slave, Equiano eventually purchased his freedom and travelled to Britain and lived the rest of his life as a prolific traveler and abolitionist. In the opening of his autobiography, Equiano expresses the same providential view common to many Black Christians on God's use of the evils of slavery to reveal the truth of the Gospel to Africans: "By the horrors of that trade was I first torn away from all the tender connexions that were naturally dear to my heart; but these, thought the mysterious ways of Providence, I ought to regard as infinitely more than compensated by the introduction

I have thence obtained to the knowledge of the Christian religion."⁵²

While Equiano reflects many African slaves who voluntarily embraced the Gospel as truth, he embraces many aspects of his native Igbo culture that correlate with biblical Israelite culture—including circumcision, the rule of judges, and the practice of burnt offerings.⁵³ Equiano became intimately familiar with Christianity but admits that he struggled with a full understanding of the Gospel. Equiano likened himself to Jacob as he wrestled with God concerning the seeming paradox of humanity's sinful incapacity to complete God's law and commensurate condemnation to eternal punishment. The law of grace as revealed in Scriptureillumined the eye of Equiano's heart as the Gospel of Christ's atonement was revealed to him during his time in London:

> I began to think I had lived a moral life, and that I had a proper ground to believe I had an interest in the divine favour; but still meditating on the subject, not knowing whether salvation was to be had partly for our own good deeds, or solely as the sovereign gift of God; in this deep consternation the Lord was pleased to break in upon my soul with his bright beams of heavenly light; and in an instant as it were, removing the veil, and letting light into a dark place, I saw clearly with the eye of faith the crucified Saviour bleeding on the cross on mount Calvary: the scriptures became an unsealed book, I saw myself a condemned criminal under the law, which came with its full force to my conscience, and "when the commandment came sin revived, and I died," I saw the Lord Jesus Christ in

his humiliation, loaded and bearing my reproach, sin, and shame."[54]

Equiano's liberation from the curse of sin through the grace of Jesus Christ engendered a missional enthusiasm for the global evangelization of the lost through the Gospel message: "I felt a deep concern for my mother and friends, which occasioned me to pray with fresh ardour and, in the abyss of thought, I viewed the unconverted people of the world in a very awful state, being without God and without hope."[55] For Equiano, liberation from social evil was not the sum of orthodox religion, as claimed by many liberation theologians. Likewise, the existence of absolute truth—realized only in the Gospel—was not a function of white supremacy but a liberating truth that empowered Blacks to fight for freedom—with no distinction between spiritual and social realities.

This was the perspective of Equiano's contemporary and fellow Black, British abolitionist Ignatius Sancho. Born a slave in the early-eighteenth century in Spanish-controlled South America, Sancho was raised in England where he composed a series of letters, many of which decried the horrors of British slavery. Along with Equiano, the truth and liberating power of the Gospel was the only adequate solution to the evils of slavery: "I am convinced that the general inhumanity of mankind proceeds...from a total indifference (if not disbelief) of the Christian faith;--a heart and mind impressed with a firm belief of the Christian tenets, must of course exercise itself in a constant uniform general philanthropy—such a being carries his heave in his breast."[56] Sancho's statement here clearly displays the biblical understanding of African Christians of the interdependency of orthodoxy and orthopraxy. Sancho and Equiano understood right relationship with Christ being inextricable from right relationship among humanity.

Equiano vigorously fought for the independence of Africans around the world using the truth of Scripture as his foundation: "Surely this traffic cannot be good, which spreads like a pestilence, and taints what it touches! Which violates that first natural right of mankind, equality and independency and gives one man a dominion over his fellows which god could never intend!"[57] Equiano's autobiography and its deployment of a biblical theology of justice and liberation were instrumental in the abolition of slavery in Britain: "May the blessings of the Lord be upon the heads of all those who commiserated the cases of the oppressed negroes, and the fear of God prolong their days; and may their expectations be filled with gladness! 'The liberal devise liberal things, and by liberal things shall stand' (Isaiah 32:8). They can say with pious Job, 'Did not I weep for him that was in trouble? Was not my soul grieved for the poor?' (Job 30:25)[58]

Equiano's younger contemporary and colleague in the Afro-British abolitionist group the Sons of Africa—Ottobah Cugoano—expressed similar condemnation of the Trans-Atlantic Slave Trade, using the Bible as his source of authority: "Surely this traffic cannot be good, which spread like a pestilence, and taints what it touches! which violates that first natural right of mankind, equality and independence and gives one man dominion over his fellows which God could never intend!"[59] In almost exactly the same words as Equiano, Cugoano criticizes pro-slavery exegesis as being guided "neither by revelation nor reason" and a "perversion" consisting of "picking out anything that will suit their purpose" and "leading them into error."[60] Cugoano then proceeds to give a comprehensive overview of Blackness and slavery in the Bible, making a pro-Black, anti-slavery exegetical argument. Cugoano understood that oppressive perversions of the Bible were false and yet praised God for saving him from the false religion of his West African upbringing through the universal Gospel of Jesus Christ:

> But, among other observations, one great duty I owe to Almighty God, (the thankful acknowledgement I would not omit for any consideration) that, although I have been brought away from my native country, in that torrent of robbery and wickedness, thanks be to God for his good providence towards me; I have both obtained liberty, and acquired the great advantages of some little learning, in being able to read and write, and, that is still infinitely of greater advantage, I trust, to know something of Him "who is that God whose providence rules over all, and who is the only Potent One that rules in the nations over the children of men. It is unto Him, who is the Prince of the Kings of the earth, that I would give all thanks. And, in some manner, I may say with Joseph, as he did with respect to the evil intention of his brethren, when they sold him into Egypt, that whatever evil intentions and bad motives those insidious robbers had in carrying me away from my native country and friends, I trust, was what the Lord intended for my good. In this respect, I am highly indebted to many of the good people of England for learning and principles unknown to the people of my native country. But, above all, what have I obtained from the Lord God of Hosts, the God of the Christians! In that divine revelation of the only true God, and the Saviour of men, what a treasure of

wisdom and blessings are involved. How wonderful is the divine goodness displayed in those invaluable books the Old and New Testaments, that inestimable compilation of books, the Bible? And, O what a treasure to have, and one of the greatest advantages to be able to read therein, and a divine blessing to understand!"[61]

The Gospel of Jesus Christ provided the theological framework for social liberation for Black theologians, ministers, and activists on both sides of the Atlantic. The heretical Christian faith in support of slavery could not thwart the *haymanot ret'et* ("orthodox") of Black Christians who easily anathematized such polluted doctrine. Such was the perspective of the abolitionist and U.S. Ambassador Frederick Douglass, the most influential African-American of the nineteenth-century. For Douglass, the inconsistency of the teachings of Scripture and the practice of white Christians in support of slavery was an indictment not against the Gospel but the doctrine of white supremacy:

> What I have said respecting and against religion, I mean strictly to apply to the slaveholding religion of this land, and with no possible reference to Christianity proper; for, between the Christianity of this land, and the Christianity of Christ, I recognize the widest possible difference—so wide, that to receive the one as good, pure, and holy, is of necessity to reject the other as bad, corrupt, and wicked. To be the friend of the one, is of necessity to be the enemy of the other. I love the pure, peaceable, and impartial Christianity of Christ: I therefore hate the corrupt, slaveholding, women-whipping, cradle-plundering, partial and

hypocritical Christianity of this land. Indeed, I can see no reason, but the most deceitful one, for calling the religion of this land Christianity."[62]

A similar attitude was reflected by Harriet Jacobs in her autobiography *Incidents in the Life of a Slave Girl*. Jacobs was born a slave in Edenton, NC, was taught to read by her initial owner and was sexually abused by her later owner James Norcom. Jacobs was educated in biblical theology which empowered her to denounce the heretical theology of her owners. Jacobs understood that the Gospel of Jesus Christ was the cornerstone of all faith and hope for African slaves: "They (slaves) never seem so happy as when shouting and singing at religious meetings. Many of them are sincere, and nearer to the gate of heaven than sanctimonious Mr. Pike, and other long-faced Christians, who see wounded Samaritans, and pass by on the other side."[63] Jacobs understood the Bible to denounce the African "trafficking of men," "selling their own children," and "violating their own daughters."[64] Jacobs more clearly understood biblical theology than her owners. When confronting her owner who was married and yet frequently raped Jacobs about his sin, he responded thusly: "His voice became hoarse with rage, 'How dare you preach to me about your infernal Bible!' he exclaimed. 'What right have you, who are my negro, to talk about what you would like, and what you wouldn't like? I am your master, and you shall obey me.' No wonder the slaves sing—

'Old Satan's church is here below;
Up to God's free church I hope to go.'"[65]

Jacobs understood the Christianity of slavery to be "Satan's church," a perverted entity distinct from "God's free church." Booker T. Washington expressed a similar perspective.

Washington was born a slave in Virginia in the 1850s and worked tirelessly to elevate and promote Black entrepreneurship—most aptly exemplified in his founding of the National Negro Business League and the Tuskegee Institute. In his autobiography *Up From Slavery*, Washington expressed the Holy Spirit's dual role of condemning the practice of slavery and using it to promote the Gospel:

> Negroes in this country, who themselves or whose forefathers went through the school of slavery, are constantly returning to Africa as missionaries to enlighten those who remained in the fatherland. This I say, not to justify slavery—on the other hand, I condemn it as an institution, as we all know that in America it was established for selfish and financial reasons, and not from a missionary motive—but to call attention to a fact, and to show how Providence so often uses men and instructions to accomplish a purpose. When persons ask me in these days how, in the midst of what sometimes seem hopelessly discouraging conditions, I can have such faith in the future of my race in this country, I remind them of the wilderness through which and out of which a good Providence has already led us.[66]

This perspective has been mirrored by countless African-American Christians throughout our history. The evils of pseudo-Christian white supremacists have for the majority of our history not obscured the pure, universal and liberating Gospel of Jesus

Christ. The careful delineation between the biblical Gospel and the syncretistic religious imagination of white supremacist American exceptionalism has constantly served as an instructive component of African and Diasporic Christianity. This remained a feature of Black theology during the advent of Pan-Africanist theological discourse of the late-nineteenth and early-twentieth centuries. Despite the common rejection of Christianity among many Pan-Africanists who reduce the totality of the Christian religion to being a mechanism of colonial oppression against African people, this was not the view of one of their foundational scholars. In a public address in the U.K. critiquing British colonialism in Africa, Marcus Garvey states:

> You have come into our homes, deceived us in every way under the guise of Christianity—but do not you ever believe I am not a Christian. I believe in God the Father, God the Son, and God the Holy Ghost; I endorse the Nicene Creed; I believe that Jesus died for me; I believe that God lives for me as for all men; and no condition you can impose on me by deceiving me about Christianity will cause me to doubt Jesus Christ and to doubt God. I shall never hold Christ or God responsible for the commercialization of Christianity by the heartless men who adopt it as the easiest means of fooling and robbing other people out of their land and country.[67]

Garvey consistently indicts the appropriation and corruption of Christianity by Western colonialism while maintaining commitment to the Gospel of Jesus Christ as revealed in Holy Scripture. The Pan-African ideological project centers around two fundamental aspects: a collective consciousness between various

African and diasporic communities and an emphasis on Black autonomy from white hegemony. Through his publication *Negro World*, his participation in the Back-to-Africa Movement through his Black Star Line, and an extensive writing and speaking career, Garvey advanced the Pan-Africanist movement throughout his native Jamaica, Britain, and the United States during the early twentieth century. Unlike its founder, many who were influenced by Garveyism in the United States increasingly understood Christianity as an outgrowth of white supremacy. One of the most significant examples of this was Malcolm X who, despite his father's Garveyian preaching that strongly denounced white supremacist Christianity, followed the trend of Noble Drew Ali, Wallace Fard Muhammad, and Elijah Muhammad in associating Christianity fundamentally with racism and oppression.

However, he was not consistent in this matter. For Malcolm was aware that white supremacist Christianity was not the totality of Church history:

> You can go right back to the very beginning of Christianity. Catholicism, the genesis of Christianity as we know it to be presently constituted, with its hierarchy, was conceived in Africa—by those whom the Christian church calls "The Desert Fathers." The Christian church became infected with racism when it entered white Europe. The Christian church returned to Africa under the banner of the Cross—conquering, killing, exploiting, pillaging, raping, bullying, beating—and teaching white supremacy.[68]

Throughout his autobiography, Malcolm is careful to add modifiers in discussing Christianity by referring to "the religion we call Christianity" and "the white man's Christianity" and the

"Holy Bible in the white man's hands and his interpretations of it" which "have been the greatest single ideological weapon for enslaving millions of non-white human beings."[69] Malcolm is absolutely correct that the movement called Christianity started by brown-skinned Palestinian Jews was significantly formed in the patristic period on the African continent and indeed became "infected" with racism in the form of an increasingly Romanized hegemonic Christianity. However, to Malcolm's point, this was not the beginning of Christianity and the ancient African and Asian expressions of Christianity continued amidst Western Christian oppression and still exist today. Even centuries of white, pseudo-Christian oppression did not completely obfuscate the reality for Malcolm that the true Gospel of Jesus Christ has nothing to do with the oppressive Christianity that built America.

Despite the increasing tendency among Pan-Africanists to reduce Christianity to being a product of Western colonialism, the roots of Pan-Africanism are found in the Ethiopian Movement of the late nineteenth century—an inherently theological and missional movement.[70] African pastors across the continent that had traditionally served in Methodist and Anglican churches began breaking away to form African Initiated Churches as a result of paternalistic European methods of governance. Western and Southern African people began seeing Ethiopia as a symbol of African ecclesiastical independence given the nation and its national

Orthodox Church having been historically independent of Western dominance. This movement was strongly motivated by the words of the psalter: "Ethiopia will quickly stretch out her hands to God" (Ps. 68:31).[71] The crucial point here is that Pan-Africanism—a movement that has drawn attention to the beauty and autonomy of people of African descent for over a century—has its roots in the theological groundwork of African churches whose movement towards African independence was motivated by the Gospel. To put it more bluntly, Black pride emerges from the Gospel of Jesus Christ.

While Christianity has been corrupted and used as a mechanism of subjugation against African-descended people for centuries, the Gospel has also been the central impetus for some of the most poignant examples of Black pride and liberation across time and place. While Dietrich Bonhoeffer experienced disillusionment over his experiences in European and white American Christianity, it was his experiences in the Black church of Harlem where he heard a complete Gospel that identified with the suffering of the cross of Christ.[72] These Black Christians that taught Bonhoeffer understood their experience to center around the crucifixion and resurrection of Jesus; not the other way around. Despite the tendency of much of contemporary Black theology to place Blackness—rather than Christ—at the center of theological discourse, this tendency would have been unthinkable for one of the most influential Black theologians in history.

Reflecting on the segregation of the American church, Howard Thurman states: "In the one place in which normal, free contacts might be most naturally established—in which the relations of the individual to his God should take priority over conditions of class, race, power, status, wealth, or the like—this place is one of the chief instruments for guaranteeing barriers."[73] Thurman shares that his grandmother would not allow him to read Pauline epistles to her because of their alleged endorsement of slavery. However, Thurman identifies this reading as a perversion of Paul by slave-owning whites and its effects on his grandmother as the motivation behind his theological work, which was aimed at correcting this perception. Thurman argues that Paul has been interpreted in "grossly misleading and inaccurate" ways and that the apostle argued clearly for an egalitarian Gospel that "transcended all barriers of race and class and condition." Furthermore, Thurman presents a holistic vision of the Gospel that, while highlighting God's identification with the oppressed, does "not ignore the theological and metaphysical interpretation of the Christian doctrine of salvation."[74]

Thurman cautions against allowing the white supremacist perversion of Christianity to become a stumbling block to the Gospel: "That it (Christianity) became, through the intervening years, a religion of the powerful and the dominant, used sometimes as an instrument of oppression, must not tempt us into believing that it was thus in the mind and life of Jesus."[75] The Gospel Haymanot that has characterized the Black Christian experience has upheld the universal lordship of Christ, lived out on earth through the Church, as a living witness to the *shalom* of God. The theological imagination of Black Christians is more than a "double-consciousness" that is defined by how Black religious discourse stands in between white individualistic piety and the social reality of Black oppression.[76] Rather, the Gospel Haymanot that has defined Black theology for nearly two millennia is a reflection of the biblical mandate to become liberated for the purpose of worshipping the triune God.

Moving Forward

The remainder of this volume will consist of various responses to and elaboration on the perspective of Gospel Haymanot. This edited volume consists of Black scholars of biblical and theological studies who are inseparably committed to the biblical orthodoxy and the liberation of Black people and all those who exist on the margins. We are children of the Black church that taught us since youth to cling tightly to the Word of God which is perfect in all it teaches. We believe that God's divine Word clearly calls for the liberation of the oppressed and highly esteems Black people as equally made in God's image. We have experienced many good things from evangelical and liberationist perspectives, yet find them disconnected from the Black Church perspective, which we call a Gospelist perspective.

Yet the holistic lived Gospel of the Black Church has largely been absent from conversations in academic theology. It is this absence that we seek to fill. This volume brings the centuries-old Gospel witness of the Black Church into theological framing which we call Gospel Haymanot. The following chapters will present specialized engagement with each scholar's academic discipline (Old Testament, New Testament, Patristics, History, Systematic Theology, Pastoral Counseling) from the perspective of Gospel Haymanot. How do we as Gospelists scholars engage our theological disciplines from the holistic perspective of the Black Church that upholds biblical orthodoxy and is committed to black flourishing? The volume will conclude with final reflections on this prolegomenon to Gospel Haymanot.

BIBLIOGRAPHY

Alexander, Michelle. *The New Jim Crow: Mass Incarceration in the Age of Colorblindness*. New York, NY: The New Press, 2010.

Anyabwile, Thabityi M. *The Decline of African-American Theology: From Biblical Faith to Cultural Captivity*. Downers Grove, IL: InterVarsity Press, 2007.

Arndt, William F., and Gingrich, F. Wilbur. *A Greek-English Lexicon of the New Testament and Other Early Christian Literature: A Translation and Adaptation of the Fourth Revised and Augmented Edition of Walter Bauer's Griechisch-Deutsches Wörterbuch zuden Schriften des Neuen Testaments und der übrigen urchristlichen Literatur*. Chicago, IL: The University of Chicago Press, 1979.

Bradley, Anthony B. *Liberating Black Theology: The Bible and the Black Experience in America*. Wheaton, IL: Crossway Books, 2010.

Brown Douglas, Kelly. *Stand Your Ground: Black Bodies and the Justice of God*. Maryknoll, NY: Orbis Books, 2015.

Cleage, Jr., Albert B. *Black Christian Nationalism: New Directions for the Black Church*. Detroit, MI: Luxor Publishers, 1987.

Cone, James H. *Black Theology and Black Power*, 7th ed. Maryknoll, NY: Orbis Books, 2005.

_____. *For My People: Black Theology and the Black Church*. Maryknoll, NY: Orbis Books, 1984.

_____. *God of the Oppressed*. Maryknoll, NY: Orbis Books, 1975.

_____. *The Cross and the Lynching Tree*. Maryknoll, NY: Orbis Books, 2011.

Cugoano, Ottobah. *Thoughts and Sentiments on the Evil and Wicked Traffic of the Slavery and Commerce of the Human Species*. Cambridge: Cambridge University Press, 2013.

Curtis IV, Edward E. and Brune Sigler, Danielle. *The New Black Gods: Arthur Huff Fauset and the Study of African American* Religions. Bloomington, IN: Indiana University Press, 2009.

Dilbeck, D.H. *Frederick Douglass: America's Prophet*. Chapel Hill, NC: University of North Carolina Press, 2018.

Douglass, Frederick. *Narrative of the Life of Frederick Douglass: An American Slave*. Cambridge: Belknap Press, 2009.

Ellis, Jr., Carl F. *Free at Last? The Gospel in the African-American Experience, 2nd ed*. Downers Grove, IL: InterVarsity Press, 1996.

Emerson, Michael O., and Smith, Christian. *Divided by Faith: Evangelical Religion and the Problem of Race in America*. Oxford: Oxford University Press, 2000.

Equiano, Olaudah. *The Interesting Narrative of the Life of Olaudah Equiano*. New York, NY: Penguin Books, 1995.

Fauset, Arthur H. *Black Gods of the Metropolis: Negro Religious Cults of the Urban North*. Philadelphia, PA: University of Pennsylvania Press, 1944.

Floyd-Thomas, Stacey, and Floyd-Thomas, Juan, and Duncan, Carol B., Ray Jr., Stephen G. and Westfield, Frazier, Franklin

E. "The Negro Church and Assimilation." In *African-American Religious Thought: An Anthology*, edited by Cornel West & Eddie S. Glaude, Jr., 62-73. Louisville, KY: Westminster John Knox, 2003.

Frederick, Marla. *Between Sundays: Black Women and Everyday Struggles of Faith*. Berkeley, CA: University of California Press, 4.

Galawdewos. *Gadla Walatta Petros*. In *The Life and Struggles of Our Mother Walatta Petros*, ed. Wendy Laura Belcher & Michael Kleiner, 119-124. Princeton: Princeton University Press, 2015.

Garvey, Marcus. "Should A Foreign Foe Invade?" In *The Marcus Garvey and Universal Negro Improvement Association Papers*, edited by Robert A. Hill, 224. Berkeley, CA: The University of California, 1990.

The Ge'ez Acts of Abba Ǝsṭifanos of G^{w}endag^{w}ende, ed. Getatchew Haile. Louvain: Secretariat du SCO, 2006.

Gerbner, Katharine. *Christian Slavery: Conversion and Race in the Protestant Atlantic World*. Philadelphia, PA: University of Pennsylvania Press, 2018.

Gilliard, Dominique Gilliard. *Rethinking Incarceration: Advocating for Justice that Restores*. Downers Grove, IL: InterVarsity Press, 2018.

Giyorgis of Segla. *Maṣḥafa Mesṭir*, ed. Yaqob Beyene. Louvain: Secretariat du SCO, 1990.

Grant, Jacquelyn. *White Women's Christ and Black Women's Jesus: Feminist Christology and Womanist Response*. Oxford: The American Academy of Religion, 1989.

Gutiérrez, Gustavo. *A Theology of Liberation: History, Politics, and Salvation*, 2nd ed. Maryknoll, NY: Orbis Books, 1988.

Jacobs, Harriet. *Incidents in the Life of a Slave Girl,* Mineola, NY: Dover Publications, 2001.

Jennings, Regina. "African Sun Imagery in the Poetry of Phillis Wheatley." *Pennsylvania English* 22, no. 1-2 (2000): 68-72.

Leslau, Wolf. *Comparative Dictionary of Ge'ez.* Wiesbaden: Harrassowitz Verlag, 2006.

Marsden, George M. *Fundamentalism and American Culture, 2nd ed.* Oxford: Oxford University Press, 2006.

Moberg, David. *The Great Reversal: Reconciling Evangelism and Social Concern, 2nd ed.* Eugene, OR: Wipf & Stock, 2006.

Oduyoye, Mercy Amba. *Introducing African Women's Theology.* Cleveland, OH: Pilgrim Press/The United Church Press, 2001.

Roberts, J. Deotis. *Liberation and Reconciliation, 2nd ed.* Louisville, KY: Westminster John Knox Press, 2005.

Sancho, Ignatius. *Letters of the Late Ignatius Sancho, An African.* New York, NY: Penguin Books, 1998.

Smith, Mark K. *Stono: Documenting and Interpreting a Southern Slave Revolt.* Columbia, SC: University of South Carolina Press, 2005.

Stevenson, Bryan. *Just Mercy: A Story of Justice and Redemption.* New York, NY: Spiegel & Grau, 2014.

Sundkler, Bengt. *Bantu Prophets in South Africa.* Cambridge: Lutterworth Press, 1948.

Thurman, Howard. *Jesus and the Disinherited.* New York, NY: Abingdon-Cokesbury Press, 1949.

_____. "Love." In *African-American Religious Thought: An*

Anthology, eds. Cornel West & Eddie S. Glaude, Jr., 49-61. Louisville, KY: Westminster John Knox Press, 2003.

Warnick, Raphael G. *The Divided Mind of the Black Church: Theology, Piety, and Public Witness*. New York, NY: New York University Press, 2014.

Washington, Booker T. *Up From Slavery: An Autobiography*. New York, NY: Doubleday, Page & Co., 1901.

Westfield, Nancy Lynne. *Black Church Studies: An Introduction*. Nashville, TN: Abingdon Press, 2007.Wheatley, Jupiter Hammon. "An Address to Miss Phillis

Wheatley, Ethiopian Poetess, in Boston, Who Came from Africa at Eight Years of Age, and Soon Became Acquainted with the Gospel of Jesus Christ." In *The Collected Works of Jupiter Hammon: Poems and Essays*, edited by Cedrick May, 11-13. Knoxville, TN: University of Tennessee Press, 2017. Wheatley, Phillis. "On Being Brought from Africa to America." In *Poems on Various Subjects, Religious and Moral*, 17. Denver, CO: W.H. Lawrence & Co., 1887.

_____. "To the Right Honourable William, Earl of Dartmouth, His Majesty's Principal Secretary of State for North America." In *Poems on Various Subjects, Religious and Moral*, 66-68. Denver, CO: W.H. Lawrence & Co., 1887.

Williams, Delores. *Sisters in the Wilderness: The Challenge of Womanist God-Talk*. Maryknoll, NY: Orbis Books, 1993.

Williams, Reggie L. *Bonhoeffer's Black Jesus: Harlem Renaissance Theology and an Ethic of Resistance*. Waco, TX: Baylor University Press, 2014.

Wolterstorff, Nicholas P. *Journey Toward Justice: Personal

Encounters in the Global South. Grand Rapids, MI: Baker Academic, 2013.

X, Malcolm. *The Autobiography of Malcolm X.* New York, NY: Random House, 1964.

Zarʻa Yaʻqob, *Mashafa Berhan.* In *The Homily of Zärʻa Yaʻəqob's* Mäṣḥafa Bərhan *on the Rite of Baptism and Religious Instruction,* ed. Getatchew Haile. Louvain: Secretariat du SCO, 2013.

1

FEMINIST, WOMANIST, AND GOSPELIST INTERPRETATIONS OF THE DAUGHTERS OF ZELOPHEHAD:
Bridging the Gap Amongst Competing Traditions

QUONEKUIA DAY

In this essay, we examine the story of the Daughters of Zelophehad from the vantage point of Feminist, Womanist and Gospelist perspectives. The goal is to provide a bridge amongst these different hermeneutics by outlining shared themes across the traditions. To uncover shared interpretations, we will compare and contrast how each approach addresses the role of four key figures in the story. The four key components are: 1.) the unmarried daughters of Zelophehad; 2.) Moses; 3.) Yahweh and his law and; 4.) the uncles. We conclude with some suggestions of how to further understand the text using a Gospel Haymanot approach. Gospel Haymanot arises out of the need to address the vacuum of theological and religious scholarship which considers themes of justice, race, and gender from an orthodox tradition. In addition, a Gospel Haymanot reclaims the voice, traditions, and experiences of Black people who are oft-neglected in the exposition of the text in orthodox settings.

The primary audience for this essay is the Black women studying within a Gospelist context. The majority of instructors at seminaries or religious institutions are Caucasian males. Rarely are Black women in these settings exposed to orthodox teaching and scholarship from other Black women. Susanne Scholz, a Feminist Biblical scholar states: "In 2001, only forty-five African American scholars held doctoral degrees in biblical studies. Eleven of them were women, eight of whom specialized in the Hebrew Bible and three in the New Testament. As a consequence, many womanist *theologians* have published womanist Bible interpretations."[77] Therefore, the challenge for the Black woman who holds to a Gospelist tradition is two-fold:

1. her academic experience is shaped and formed by mostly white-male instructors and;
2. the image that reflects her in academia may be at odds with her theology.

We begin our investigation into the Daughters of Zelophehad with an overview of the story in Numbers 27 and 36. We follow with a review of the account according to the Feminist, Womanist and Gospelist traditions. Then, we outline the shared content and conclude with some suggestions on reading the text according to Gospel Haymanot.

Daughters of Zelophehad in Numbers 27 and Numbers 36

In Numbers 27:1-9, five unmarried daughters of Zelophehad—Mahlah, Noah, Hoglah, Milkah, and Tirzah—request a land inheritance from their uncles to preserve their father's name. Zelophehad is a descendant of Manasseh. Manasseh was born to Joseph and his African wife, Asenath, the daughter of Potipherah (son of Re), the priest of On.[78] The five daughters of Zelophehad approach Moses and the elders and present the case: their father died for his own sins and had no sons. Consequently, there is no male heir to preserve the family name and inherit their portion of the promised land. The women demand to have an inheritance so their father's name will not be cut off from the community of Israel. Moses brings the case to Yahweh, symbolizing the uniqueness and complexity of the petition. In the Israelite community, only sons were allowed to inherit their father's land. Scholars differ on whether the women of the surrounding nations could inherit. David L. Stubbs argues Egyptian women inherited land and Timothy Ashley asserts there were cases of women inheriting in the second and third millennia.[79] Louis Ndekha describes the inheritance law as "bad" and contends that Yahweh copies other nations by restricting women from inheriting.[80] Ndekha's perception of Yahweh is precarious since Yahweh intends to distinguish himself and the Israelites from the practices of other nations. Yahweh responds to Moses: *kên bənōwṯ ṣəlāp̄ əḥāḏ dōḇərōṯ* ("the daughters of Zelophehad speak right") and orders him to give them an inheritance (27:6-7). Ironically, Yahweh's response does not include a recognition of Zelophehad's name (a concern of the daughters), only that the women can inherit and the order of inheritance. The new law allows for daughters to receive property in cases where there is no son and for the daughter's inheritance to precede the father's brothers and uncles. The new order of inheritance results in a status change for the daughters; they are now their deceased father's nearest relative. The story in Numbers 27 concludes with the women winning their case; they can inherit their father's land. Significantly, the amended law applies to the entire Israelite community; all women in families with no sons can receive an inheritance and maintain the family name.

In Numbers 36:1-13, the daughter's uncles challenge the law on the basis that the tribe of Manasseh will lose land if the women marry outside of their tribe. Moses affirms the uncle's case and answers: *'al pî Yhvh* ("according to the mouth of the Lord" - 36:6), the women who inherit must marry within their tribe. Wilda Gafney argues this response from Moses is not from Yahweh, but Moses alone, because it is not a direct divine address.[81] Although Numbers 36 does not include a divine address from Yahweh to Moses nor a repetition of that speech from Moses to the Israelites, it does repeat in four out of the thirteen verses that Moses was following the commandment of Yahweh. Numbers 36:5 records that Moses speaks *'al pî Yhvh* ("according to the mouth of the Lord"), in v. 6 *zeh haddāḇār* ʾăšer *ṣiwwāh Yhvh* ("This is the word which the Lord commanded"), in v. 10 the daughters do *ka'ăšer ṣiwwāh Yhvh eth mōšeh* ("according to which the Lord commanded to Moses"), and v.13 ʾēl·leh *hammiṣwōṯ wəhammišpāṭîm* ʾăšer *ṣiwwāh Yhvh* ("these are the commandments which the Lord commanded").

Feminist, Womanist, and Gospelist Interpretations

Feminist biblical criticism has its foundation in the works of Elizabeth Cady Stanton, Phyllis Trible, Esther Fuchs, and

Elisabeth Schüssler Fiorenza.[82] Feminist biblical critics' goals are to reclaim women's voices, status, and justice in the biblical text. They argue that the biblical text is androcentric and written with a patriarchal agenda.[83] Helen Schüngel-Straumann maintains that "the Bible has always been read and interpreted *selectively*, often abusing the Bible to fortify the bastions of male dominance."[84] Schüngel-Straumann, as other Feminist biblical critics, approaches the Bible with suspicion, raising questions concerning the historicity and inerrancy of the text.[85]

Womanist biblical interpretation has its roots in the works of Alice Walker, Audre Lorde, Maya Angelou, Renita Weems, Katie Cannon, Jacquelyn Grant, and Delores Williams.[86] Womanist biblical interpretation expands the themes addressed by the Feminist biblical critic to include issues of race, classism, post-colonialism, and images of sexuality.[87] Williams offers four distinctions between Womanist and Feminist biblical criticism: "1. in various cultural contexts, understanding the meaning of 'what is acceptably female'; 2. the scope and definition of the term patriarchy; 3. different and sometimes opposing hermeneutical positions; 4. different responses to the question: What can we say about God's relation to the oppressed in history?"[88] In evaluating category one, what is acceptably female, Williams explores how the image of the New Testament Mary as a small white woman does not reflect the Black Woman. In fact, what a white Mary represents is more in line with the oppressive slave mistress than a Black woman. The Womanist represents every woman of color and the obstacles they endure living in not only a white male-dominant world, but any context which rejects the humanity and presence of the Black Woman.

The Gospelist approach centers on recovering the authorial intent and understanding the text as historical and inerrant. It is akin to the historical-grammatical or grammatico-historical method. The historical-grammatical method developed in response to the allegorical tradition employed by the Catholic Church. The allegorical approach assumes there is more than a singular meaning to a text. In contrast, the historical-grammatical critic searches for the original meaning of the text as intended by the author. Raymond Surburg argues the historical-grammatical approach holds fifteen presuppositions concerning the text. We have included five of them in this essay. They are as follows: "1) the Bible is the word of God; 2) the canonical books do not include the Apocrypha; 3) the meaning of the text can only be determined from the original language; 4) the Bible is the final authority, not the church; 5) the literal meaning is the preferred."[89] The crux of the historical- grammatical method is to determine the author's intent for the Biblical record. This is achieved through an exegetical process to decide the historical context of the passage and the original meaning of the words. The Biblical account, including sites and persons, is regarded as a historical record of events as experienced by the persons in the text.

However, not everyone in the text receives equal evaluation by those who hold to a Gospelist tradition. This may be in part due to a limitation of the scholar or a scholar's goal to advance themes which center on Yahweh and the heroes of the text. For example, in Genesis 21:14, Abraham sends away his African slave Hagar and their child Ishmael. He does so at the command of his wife (Gn. 21:10) and in obedience to Yahweh (Gn. 21:12-13). Scholars who embrace a Gospelist reading famously contend Ishmael must leave in order to preserve the covenant with Isaac. Ishmael represents a fruitless future, and Abraham was simply obeying Yahweh.[90] The Evangelical reading rarely wrestles with what it means to Hagar and Ishmael to be abandoned by Abraham and Sarah, the injustice of being sent into a wilderness with little food and water and no escort, or what the text reveals about Yahweh who saves Hagar and Ishmael, promising the non-covenantal child a prosperous future. All of these characters and events require attention from a Gospelist tradition, not just the heroes of faith.

The content of the biblical text differs across Feminist, Womanist, and Gospelist traditions. The Gospelist approach accepts the Bible as a closed canon of 66 books, 39 in the Old Testament and 27 in the New Testament. The Feminist and Womanist biblical critics reference the 66 books along with the Apocrypha and Midrash in the evaluation of the text.[91] In our analysis of the Daughters of Zelophehad, we will note if scholars reference the Midrash or Apocrypha in the interpretation of the text.

Feminist and Womanist Interpretation of the Daughters of Zelophehad Story

Sakenfeld

Just over 30 years ago, Katharine Sakenfeld penned an essay on the Zelophehad Daughters in response to the "inattention" given to story.[92] She argued there were a series of "problems" in the Numbers 27 and 36 account of these women who petition for a land inheritance. One problem was the structure of the narrative. In Numbers 27, the women win their petition for land and thus maintain their father's name. In Numbers 36, the uncles challenge the petition on the grounds that they may lose tribal property when the women marry outside their tribe. Sakenfeld found it problematic that the uncles' challenge occurs in Numbers 36, nine chapters after the initial petition. She further questioned whether the account in Numbers 36 was evidence that the chapter is from a later author or an indication that the uncles did not immediately understand the consequences of the new law. Sakenfeld draws attention to the silence of the Daughters of Zelophehad after they successfully argue for a land inheritance. Sakenfeld imagines the response of the women and then "invites" the reader to imagine it as well, thereby giving "voice" to the unusual silence in the text.[93]

In Numbers 36, Sakenfeld recognizes a problem with the uncles' challenge to the petition. The uncles are concerned with the loss of the inherited land if the Daughters of Zelophehad marry outside of their tribe. They argue that even the Jubilee Law could not reverse the change. The Jubilee Law allowed land transferred to another tribe to return to the original tribe after 50 years (Lv. 25:23-28). Sakenfeld posits that the uncles' reference to the year of Jubilee tradition does not apply to the condition of the Daughters of Zelophehad. She maintains that Jubilee Law does not account for inherited land but sold land.

In another essay on the Daughters of Zelophehad, Sakenfeld uses the story as a framework to explore the state of Feminist critical reading of the biblical text.[94] She presents three ways of translating the text based on three methods used by Feminist scholars: 1.) "formal literary approach;" 2.) "discourse analysis;" and 3.) "historical inquiry rather than literary study."[95] She contends that the Feminist biblical scholar can arrive at very different interpretations depending on the methodology. She concludes with a mandate for biblical Feminists to engage more often with other biblical Feminists who employ different methodologies.

Now we turn to the four key themes of the story to make some observations on how Sakenfeld interacts with each component: 1.) the five unmarried daughters of Zelophehad; 2.) Moses; 3.) Yahweh and his law and; 4.) the uncles. Sakenfeld opines that the women are brave because they approach Moses and the elders, but restricted through the marriage stipulation in Numbers 36. She understands the role of Moses as one who obeys Yahweh in the first emendation of the law in Numbers 27, but rules independent of Yahweh's commands in Numbers 36. She argues that Yahweh gives the original land inheritance law not anticipating the problem of a family without a male heir. The uncles are "unhappy" with the amended law and represent a patriarchal system, attempting to maintain power in spite of Yahweh's ruling.[96]

Claassens

Juliana Claassens examines the story of the Daughters of Zelophehad from the vantage points of gender criticism and post-colonial interpretation. She argues that the Feminist biblical critics frequently find themselves having to address both areas when evaluating a text. For the gender critic, the Daughters of Zelophehad represent the plight of women maneuvering through patriarchal systems.[97] However, women in the post-colonial interpretation represent both victim and oppressor. For example, in the Daughters of Zelophehad story, the gender critic highlights the daughters' vulnerable state and how they seek justice in a system slanted favorably towards the men. The Daughters in the post-colonial interpretation are vulnerable, yet complicit with the male- dominant patriarchal system that willingly takes the land of other people groups. Claassens asserts that when Yahweh affirms the women's petition, it reveals that his law is insufficient. Claassens recommends the Feminist critic read the text observing the "human dignity" of each group while using either methodology. She states that "cultivating compassion for the other would thus requires an act of resistant reading that challenges this deep-seated ideology embedded in the biblical traditions."[98] For Claassens, to accept post-colonial interpretation is to reject the biblically orthodox presentation of the "other" as non-covenant people worthy of expulsion.

Four Key Themes: Claassen argues that the Daughters of Zelophehad are bold, courageous, and insightful (who see what Yahweh does not) women who become "a symbol of the powerless standing up for what is right."[99] Moses is the intermediary who hears the appeal of the daughters, but in the second amendment in Numbers 36, he does not fully understand how to apply the newly amended law of inheritance to the Daughters of Zelophehad. Claassen's assessment of Moses relies heavily on the Midrash which presents Moses as unprepared for the uncles' request in Numbers 36. Yahweh and his law are flawed because of not anticipating a sonless family. The uncles represent those who are obstacles to Yahweh's just ruling on behalf of the Daughters of Zelophehad.

Shemesh

Yael Shemesh explores the story of the Daughters of Zelophehad from three fields of study: gender perspective, Midrash, and Feminist Midrash. In her estimation of the text, she discovers how the interpretation of the story changes from one that is androcentric to one that becomes more focused on the needs of the Daughters of Zelophehad.[100] Following the gender perspective, Shemesh believes this story features women, but does not focus on the needs of women. She argues that this account of the Daughters of Zelophehad is not a feminist story. Shemesh states that the multiple references to "'son' 5 times in its opening verse," use of a "paternal genealogy," and the repetition of the daughters' names are reminders to the reader that Zelophehad is sonless—so it "serves a patriarchal goal."[101] She contends that in the Midrash, the Feminist interpretation that the divine law is flawed is corrected. She claims that "it had always been his [God] intention that the daughters inherit in the absence of sons. For various reasons (to teach Moses a lesson or to reward Joseph), however, this *halakhah* was withheld from Moses and God permitted Zelophchad's daughters to be responsible for its promulgation."[102] The law is not the problem in the Midrash, it is Moses' limitations which are problematic. In the Midrash, the women are honored for their love of the land and their petition for justice. In the Feminist Midrash, the women are lauded for their collective work in the presentation of their appeal. In Shemesh's essay, the Daughters of Zelophehad, according to a gender perspective, are bold and courageous.

Four Key Themes: In Midrash and Feminist Midrash, the women are more knowledgeable than Moses because Moses failed to directly petition Yahweh. Yahweh and his law are flawed in the gender tradition. In the Midrash and Feminist Midrash, neither Yahweh nor his law are the emphasis of the failure, but Yahweh is more merciful than man. In the Midrash and Feminist Midrash, Moses lacks discernment and understanding. In the gender approach, Moses adheres to the concerns of the uncles. The uncles are oppressive in gender perspective. In the Midrash and Feminist Midrash, the uncles do not represent those who care for the proper allotment of the promised land.

Gafney

Gafney engages the story of the Daughters of Zelophehad in Numbers 27 and 36 using Womanist Midrash. Gafney begins by outlining the importance of calling the daughters by their names: Mahlah, Noah, Hoglah, Milkah, and Tirzah, honoring the African naming tradition and reclaiming the loss of the name for the millions of Africans who suffered through the trans-Atlantic Slave Trade. She suggests that these women's names occur more often than any other women's names in the Bible. She points to their bravery and the collective approach with which they present their case to Yahweh and Yahweh's affirmation of their petition: "In a truly rare move in Scriptures, their story is an explicit affirmation of women's agency and resistance to patriarchy by God."[103] Gafney has sharp criticism for Moses who she describes as one benefiting from women who preserved his life but then works against the Daughters of Zelophehad by connecting their inheritance to a marriage requirement: "Moses' use of his power and authority to disenfranchise women in his community identifies him as one of the male religious leaders in virtually every religious tradition of which I have ever heard whose response to women's demands for equality—even a small amount of parity—is, 'Over my dead body.'"[104] She believes the role of the uncles is equally discriminatory as they represent the challenge to the divine law instituted by Yahweh. For Gafney, the groundbreaking role of the women has relevance for the women in Israel and the modern-day reader.

Four Key Themes: The women survive the multiple obstacles of a flawed law and confront the injustice of their circumstances. Gafney acknowledges Yahweh's affirmation of the women as positive for the women, but then criticizes Yahweh for transitioning from command language to more passive grammar in the declaration of the new inheritance law.[105] Moses is credited for bringing the women's petition to Yahweh, but chided for adding a stipulation of marriage for land inheritance. She understands the uncles as those who desire to maintain an anthrocentric community.

Gospelist Tradition

Cole

R. Dennis Cole explores the development of case law as it is presented in the story of the Daughters of Zelophehad. He describes the significance of land inheritance, stating a loss of land was evidence of "divine judgment and eventual societal abandonment."[106] He argues that living without a land inheritance was "grave" and required action.[107] But, the gravity extends to other practical concerns for the Daughters of Zelophehad. They had to confront the genuine possibility of entering the promised land without a place to call home. Cole argues that the women present their father's legacy as one deserving of an inheritance because "he died of his own sins." He notes the daughters' case is "precedent-setting,"[108] since no woman had yet to challenge the land inheritance law. Cole points to the use of Moses and the council as a precursor to the role of Midrash for Jewish believers. For Cole, the case law is unflawed but develops when cases are brought before Moses and elders. In the Daughters of Zelophehad account, Yahweh answers in the affirmative to preserve a land inheritance for Zelophehad. In Numbers 36, Cole contends the concern of the uncles is they may lose the land they fought for and deemed profitable:

> The Machirites had acquired this territory by force from the Amorites in the region of Gilead because the land was desirable for the pasturage of their herds and flocks—not only by the Machirites but also by the entire tribes of Gad and Reuben (32:1-28). Assuming the Machirites had agreed to support the other tribes in the conquest of Canaan, as had the Gadites and Reubenites, Moses granted this clan the Gilead region because they defeated and disposed the Amorites who had been living in that region.[109]

Therefore, the concern of the uncles from Gilead was not just tribal property allotment but it was a personal interest in preserving a specific territory.

Four Key Themes: Cole describes the Daughters of Zelophehad as "pious" and "obedient" women who come before the council with an "attitude of supplication."[110] He hails their ability to act in the presence of an all-male council. Moses is a "quality spiritual leader" because he turns to Yahweh for guidance.[111] Cole understands Yahweh as the God who fulfills his promise to provide land for his children. Yahweh's law is "precedent-setting" because it allows women to inherit in cases where there is no male heir. He maintains the uncles' petition reveals a desire to keep their own property.

Brown

Raymond Brown's analysis of the story of the Daughters of Zelophehad is set within a series of themes that he argues are present throughout the book of Numbers. It is apparent that Brown envisions his audience to be those who share a common tradition as each theme points to establishing or reinforcing a relationship with Yahweh. For example, one is "Trust the Lord." [112] Under this heading, he addresses the Daughters' bold presentation before the council and the importance of the land inheritance. Then he suggests that onlookers would have been encouraged to maintain faith, having observed the women's demand for the land they had yet to possess. Sakenfeld offers an alternate picture of the audience: "But one may imagine the responses of the onlookers (shock, amazement, incredulity) and play with the adjectives they may have whispered to one another concerning these women—foolhardy, daring, assertive, aggressive….Did someone perhaps whisper more softly 'justified?'"[113] In another theme, "Seek the Lord's Help," Brown suggests that Yahweh always intended for the women to inherit, and the limitation to a male heir was done to prompt Moses to turn to him for guidance.[114] Brown also explores the uncles' request to have the law further amended in Numbers 36 under additional thematic headings. He posits the uncles' petition is an example of them maintaining proper "stewardship" over the Promised Land.[115] Brown argues that a disproportionate allocation of land to one tribe over the other is poor stewardship of the resources Yahweh has granted his people.

Four Key Themes: Brown contends the women represent faith in Yahweh's promises. They have waited for Yahweh to fulfill his promise and now the time has come for the Israelites to receive their inheritance. Moses is a faithful leader because he turns to God for guidance for a complex case. Yahweh is trustworthy and his laws encourage faithfulness and obedience. The uncles are careful stewards desirous of protecting the fair allotment of the covenantal land.

Stubbs

In the analysis of the Daughters of Zelophehad story, Stubbs takes special care to observe the meaning revealed in the structure of the book of Numbers. He argues this based on the fact that the Daughters of Zelophehad is the first story after the wilderness where the people can prove they will be different from the former generation.[116] He describes the uniqueness of the Daughters' direct challenge to Yahweh, as opposed to contemporary accounts where the challenge would be directed at a body of leaders. Surprisingly, Yahweh agrees with the daughters' petition and issues a new decree that any woman in a situation such as the daughters' would be able to inherit land. Stubbs considers why Yahweh prohibits daughters from inheriting, since other nations allowed single women to inherit. He then responds to his own question, "If the land were equally distributed to both sons and daughters upon their parents' death, marriages between tribes would quickly dissolve the tribal land system."[117] In his questioning of Yahweh's purpose, he does not ask why Yahweh awaits the challenge to the law, as opposed to including the stipulation in the initial inheritance law. Stubbs continues that Yahweh's answer is affirming of the women because it is fair to the tribe. It allows for them to have "economic independence" and indicates the care of the women outweighing "male privilege."[118] For Numbers 36, Stubbs does not mention the uncles and their petition to Moses. Rather, he argues that the "problem is solved" (i.e., the threat to the patriarchal line) when the daughters adhere to the command to marry within their tribe.

Four Key Points: Stubbs notes that the Daughters are bold advocates who petition to maintain the patriarchal line. Moses is faithful to bring the case to Yahweh for council. Yahweh gives an inheritance law that addresses the needs of the women and later the uncles. The uncles' only concern is to not lose any of their inheritance.

Martin

Glen Martin's analysis of the Daughters of Zelophehad story is more of a summary of events than an exegetical exploration of the story. For Numbers 27, he presents the challenge of the daughters—their father died and left no male heirs to carry forward the family name. His discussion of Moses is limited to what Moses does—brings a difficult case to Yahweh who grants the daughters' request. Martin does not mention the affirmation of the women by Yahweh or the possibility that this divine law was successfully challenged. There is no reference to the land, the covenant promise, not even the listing of the daughters' names or the bravery required of them to petition for land. Martin notes that Moses, in Numbers 36, affirms the uncles and that the new law is an example of how Yahweh cares for the vulnerable and underprivileged.[119] Ironically, the uncles who have the least amount to lose in the story are referred to by Martin as "affirmed" in their request for another emendation of the inheritance law.

Four Key Points: For Martin, the Daughters are women who desire to maintain their father's name and so request an inheritance. Who they are aside from children of Zelophehad or their efforts as a collective to challenge divine law are not addressed. Moses is the obedient leader of Israel. Yahweh changes the law in Numbers 27 and Numbers 36 to give an inheritance to his children, and the uncles are validated for their request to revise the law.

Bridging the Gap

In this essay, our goal was to explore the story of the Daughters of Zelophehad in Feminist, Womanist, and Gospelist traditions to determine if there were any shared principles that could be gleaned from these competing traditions. This was done by reviewing the story within each tradition with an eye toward four key components: 1.) the Daughters of Zelophehad; 2.) Moses; 3.) Yahweh and His Law and; 4.) the uncles. In the review of the story there was broad agreement in three of the four components of the story. However, the details which led to the shared theme sometimes differed across traditions. We address each one in turn.

1. The Daughters of Zelophehad: Honored for Their Bravery and Boldness

In the Feminist, Womanist, and Gospelist approaches, the women were highly regarded for their victorious petition before the council. In the Feminist and Womanist traditions, the daughters' stance was framed as a victory against oppressive policy based on gender. Also, they noted the women's victory was likely tempered by the mandate to marry in Numbers 36. As for the Gospelist tradition, the Daughters of Zelophehad were applauded for their bravery, boldness, and obedience. The Daughters of Zelophehad's stance and ensuing obedience showed that they were not like the wilderness tradition—they obeyed Moses and Yahweh. Feminist/Womanist scholars noted the silence of the women after their victory and imagined their joyous reaction and voice. Neither the voice nor reaction were noted by the representative of the Gospelist tradition. Rather, attention was drawn to the impact of the new law for the family of Zelophehad and the tribe of Manasseh.

2. Moses: Moses Applauded for His Leadership in Numbers 27

Feminist/Womanist scholars typically applauded Moses for his initial response in Numbers 27 but question his decision-making in Numbers 36. For Gospelists, Moses is a faithful leader who knows how to respond to complex legal cases. For example, Moses brought the problematic case in Numbers 27 to Yahweh. For the less complex Numbers 36, he answered according to what was already revealed to him by Yahweh.

3. Yahweh and His Law: Yahweh Applauded for His Willingness to Change His Law

Feminist, Womanist, and Gospelist traditions applaud Yahweh for changing his law. The Feminists/Womanists celebrate Yahweh for the new law, public affirmation of the women, and commanding the communication of the new law to all the Israelites. The new law changes the status of all unmarried women in families with no male heir. The unmarried daughter becomes her father's nearest relative; she can carry the family name and have economic independence (until marriage). For Gospelists, Yahweh is applauded for his faithfulness to Israel. He provides an inheritance to women to ensure fair allotment of the land.

4. The Uncles: General Disagreement on the Role of the Uncles

For the Feminist/Womanist perspective, the uncles were universally denounced as obstacles to the newly amended law. In the Gospelist readings, the uncles were presented as wanting to maintain their land and not having an alternate agenda to oppose the daughters' inheritance.

A Gospel Haymanot to Reading of the Daughters of Zelophehad: Why a Gospel Haymanot?

A Gospel Haymanot addresses themes of justice, race, and gender often found in liberal traditions, such as Feminist/Womanist biblical readings from the vantage point of orthodoxy. In this story of the Daughters of Zelophehad, we propose four themes which advance a reading of a Gospel Haymanot. They are as follows:

1. **Read the Names of Persons and Regions They Occupy and Previously Occupied**

In the historic T.V. series *Roots*, a young slave boy is outstretched hanging with his wrists tightly bound with rope. The white master has a Black slave man whip the young slave boy across his back. After the crack of another whip, the white master asks the young slave boy, "What's your name?" The young slave boy replies, "My name is Kunta Kinte." The slave boy resists over and over again and each time he is whipped. Then there is the final moment, the slave master after a series of whips asks the young slave boy once again "what is your name?" and the slave boy answers, "My name is Toby." This heartbreaking moment of the series was more than a master trying to re- name Kunta Kinte. African-Americans who understood the meaning of that scene knew it was not merely a beating; the white slave master tried to strip Kuna Kinte of his manhood, his Blackness, his identity, his family, his tribe, his country, his heritage, his language, his being as a man created in the image of God. Names for African-Americans are not what we are called, alone, but the name reflects who we are as a people. If Mahlah, Noah, Hoglah, Milkah, and Tirzah are in the text and we know their forefather—Joseph—married an African woman named Asenath, then we should call out their names. We should reintroduce them to the ones who now hear and study the word of God.

2. **Emphasize Working as a Collective**

The Daughters and the Uncles each are successful in their petition to amend the law. The greatest moments in Black history have come as a result of Black people working together to fight against injustices. The Civil Rights Movement, which included desegregation of schools, voting rights, right to health care, and access to loans for housing and businesses, only happened when Black people came together to oppose injustices.

3. **Emphasize Complex Leadership**

Leaders are complex and this is not a disqualifier for leadership. Feminists/Womanists affirm Moses' role in Numbers 27 but then wrestle with accepting his actions in Numbers 36. Black sports figures, politicians, ministers, entertainers who have failed on some level are not abandoned by many Black people because they share the commonness of race and ethnicity.

4. **Reinforce Promises**

The women approach Moses with an expectation that Yahweh will keep his promise to his people, and they receive a positive response to their request. Black Christians embrace a theology of Yahweh as faithful and one who keeps his promises. This theology is evident in the historic Black National Anthem, "Lift Every Voice and Sing," a portion of the lyrics read:

> Sing a song full of the faith that the dark past has taught us

Sing a song full of the hope that the present has brought us

Facing the rising sun of our new day begun
Let us march on 'til victory is won

Black Christians embrace a theology that God rescues the poor and afflicted and does not forget his promises to his covenant people.

BIBLIOGRAPHY

Angelou, Maya. *The Heart of a Woman*. New York, NY: Random House, 1981.

Ashley, Timothy. *The Book of Numbers*. New International Commentary on the Old Testament Series. Grand Rapids, MI: Eerdmans Publishing, 1993.

Brown, Raymond. *The Message of Numbers: Journey to the Promised Land*. Downers Grove, IL: InterVarsity Press, 2002.

Byron, Gay, and Lovelace, Vanessa. *Womanist Interpretations of the Bible: Expanding the Discourse*. Atlanta, GA: SBL Press, 2016.

Cannon, Katie. *Katie's Canon: Womanism and the Soul of the Black Community*. New York, NY: Continuum, 1995.

Claassens, Juliana. "Give us a Portion Among our Father's Brothers': The Daughters of Zelophehad, Land, and the Quest for Human Dignity." *JSOT* 37 (2013): 319-37.

Cole, R. Dennis. *Numbers*. NAC. Nashville, TN: B&H Publishing, 2000.

Fiorenza, Elisabeth. *Wisdom Ways: Introducing Feminist Biblical Interpretation*. Maryknoll, NY: Orbis Books, 2001.

Fuchs, Esther. *Sexual Politics in the Biblical Narrative: Reading the Hebrew Bible as a Woman*. New York: NY Sheffield Academic Press, 2000.

Gafney, Wilda. *Womanist Midrash: A Reintroduction to the Women of the Torah and the Throne*. Louisville, KY: Westminster John

Knox Press, 2017.

Grant, Jacquelyn. *White Women's Christ and Black Women's Jesus.* New York, NY: Oxford University Press, 1989.

Junior, Nyasha. *An Introduction to Womanist Biblical Interpretation.* Louisville, KY: Westminster John Knox Press, 2015.

Kidner, Derek. *Genesis.* Tyndale Old Testament Commentary Series. Downers Grove, IL: InterVarsity Press, 2019.

Lorde, Audre. *Sister Outsider: Essays and Speeches.* Berkeley, CA: The Crossing Press, 1984.

Martin, Glen and Anders, Max. *Holman Old Testament Commentary.* Nashville, TN: Broadman & Holman Publishers, 2002.

Ndekha, Louis. "The Daughters of Zelophehad and African Women's Rights: A Malawian Perspective on the Book of Numbers 27:1-11." *AJGR* 19, no. 2 (2013): 37-51.

Sakenfeld, Katharine. "Zelophehad's Daughter's." *PRST* 15 (1988): 37-47.

⎯⎯⎯⎯. "In the Wilderness, Awaiting the Land: The Daughters of Zelophehad and Feminist Interpretation." *PSB* 9 (1988): 179-86.

Scholz, Susanne. "Stirring Up Vital Energies: Feminist Biblical Studies in North America (1980s- 2000s)." In *Feminist Biblical Studies in the Twentieth Century: Scholarship and Movement,* edited by Fiorenza, Elisabeth Schüssler, 53-70. Atlanta: Society of Biblical Literature, 2014.

⎯⎯⎯⎯. *Introducing the Women's Hebrew Bible: Feminism, Gender Justice, and the Study of the Old Testament.* London: Bloomsbury T&T, 2017.

Schüngel-Straumann, Helen. "Genesis 1-11 The Primordial History." In *Feminist Biblical Interpretation: A Compendium of Critical Commentary on the Books of the Bible and Related Literature*, edited by Luise Schottroff and Marie-Theres Wacker, 1-14. Grand Rapids, MI: William B. Eerdmans, 2012.

Shemesh, Yael. "A Gender Perspective on the Daughters of Zelophehad: Bible, Talmudic Midrash, and Modern Feminist Midrash." *BibInt* 15 (2007): 80-109.

Smith, Mitzi J. *I Found God in Me: A Womanist Biblical Hermeneutics Reader*. Eugene, OR: Cascade Books, 2015.

Stanton, Elizabeth C. *The Woman's Bible* part 1. New York, NY: European Publishing, 1895. Stubbs, David L. *Numbers*. Brazos Theological Commentary on the Bible Series. Grand Rapids, MI: 2009.

Surburg, Raymond F. "The Presuppositions of the Historical-Grammatical Method as Employed by Historic Lutheranism." *The Springfielder* 38, no. 4 (1974): 278-88.

Trible, Phyllis. *Texts of Terror: Literary-Feministic Readings of Biblical Narratives*. Philadelphia, PA: Fortress Press, 1984.

Walker, Alice. *In Search of Our Mothers' Gardens: Womanist Prose*. New York, NY: Harcourt, 1983.

Weems, Renita. *Just a Sister Away*. Philadelphia, PA: Innisfree Press, 1988.

Williams, Delores. *Sisters in the Wilderness: The Challenge of Womanist God-Talk*. Maryknoll, NY: Orbis Books, 1993.

2

GRACE REVERSED:
The Significance and Application of Amos' Reuse of Exodus and Conquest Motifs

CLEOTHA ROBERTSON

The purpose of this paper is to examine the use of Exodus themes and Conquest motifs in the book of Amos. Additionally, this paper will examine these motifs as utilized by Amos in his context. Finally, I will conclude with a list of theological conclusions, implications, and personal reflections regarding Amos' appropriation of the Exodus and Conquest themes. These conclusions concern the implications of Amos' re-contextualization of Exodus motifs and Conquest themes for Old Testament hermeneutics. My reflections as a Gospelist scholar will attempt to contextualize the significance of Amos to my own context. Additionally, I will also reflect upon these implications for "scholars of color" who are concerned about the development of a "Gospel Haymanot ('Theology')." Gospel

Haymanot is the perspective that maintains a high view of scripture coupled with biblical justice from a Black perspective.

The Book of Amos: Context and Outline

Amos is one of the five prophets of the Neo-Assyrian Period along with Jonah, Hosea, Micah, and Isaiah. According to Amos 1:1, Amos is a prophet from Tekoa, located about six miles south of Bethlehem in the Judean hills. Amos is called from his pastoral occupation to one of the flourishing urban centers of the Northern Kingdom. With Amos, Hebrew prophecy reaches a new plateau. Amos is the first of the writing prophets since Moses who links the welfare and survival of the nation to the moral obedience of the people of Israel. Amos prophesied during the reigns of Uzziah (791-740) in the South and Jeroboam II (793-753) in the North. The ministry of Amos to the Northern Kingdom of Israel occurs sometime between 767 and 753 BCE. The mention of Amos' prophetic ministry transpiring two years before the earthquake that has been dated by Yadin in his excavation of Hazor as occurring in 760 BCE, aids in confirming potential dates of the prophecies of Amos.[120]

The book of Amos is a short book consisting of only nine chapters. According to the Masorah at the end of the Hebrew manuscript, there are 146 verses.[121] By word count, the book contains about 2,053 words. The book contains eight diverse ingredients: judgment oracles against nations, exhortations, plagues, hymns, woe oaths, visions, and eschatology.

The book of Amos can be outlined in the following manner:
Part 1: Judgment on the Nations (1:1 - 2:16)
Part 2: Oracles Concerning Israel (3:1 - 6:14)
Part 3: Visions and Exhortations (7:1 - 9:16)

Amos and the Reuse of Exodus Theme and Conquest Themes

Gary V. Smith, in his article "Continuity and Discontinuity in Amos' Use of Tradition," notes prophetic oracle continuity with the past by referencing God's mighty deeds or alluding to ancient Israelite literary tradition.[122] Exodus and Conquest traditions are used prominently in Amos. The writer will examine some of these passages in Amos. More specifically, the writer will examine how Amos re-contextualizes Exodus materials and Conquest motifs to address his eighth-century context. Amos references incidents from the book of Exodus, other Pentateuchal themes, and historical occurrences described in Joshua. These important incidents recall the manner in which Yahweh has interacted with the Children of Israel. The citing of these historical incidents raises hermeneutical concerns. Among these are the following: Which events in Amos' prophecies are referenced? How are these events reused in Amos? How does the recollection of these events differ from the actual events as recounted earlier? How are we to understand the historicity of these events based upon the recollection of them in Amos?

The following are passages in Amos that mention Exodus themes. The writer lists six specific passages that deal with themes from the book of Exodus. These passages are 3:1-2, 5:7-8, 5:12, 7:7-9, 8:8-10, and 9:7-8. The themes can be classified in the following three categories. One passage deals with the casuistic laws found in Exodus 21-23. Three passages mention the Plagues on Egypt. Two passages reference the Exodus event itself. One of the passages that recounts the Exodus also references the Conquest of Canaan. From the perspective of Gospel Haymanot, it is notable that Amos' concerns—which are echoes of the Exodus and Conquest narratives—reflect Yahweh's inseparable concern for proper worship and equitable social relations for His People.

Exodus Passages and Conquest Passages in Amos

1. Amos 3:1, 2

3:1 "Listen, you Israelites, to this message which the Lord is proclaiming against you! This message is for the entire clan I brought up from the land of Egypt.

3:2 I have chosen you alone from all the clans of the earth. Therefore I will punish you for all your sins."[123]

Amos 3:1 and 2 reference the Exodus event. Amos 3:1 and 2 form a short oracle delivered by Amos that serves as an introduction to oracles against Israel that one finds in Amos 3-6.[124] Amos 3:1 and 2 are a component of the larger subunit of 3:1-15. This larger section of the oracle lists the cause of God's punishment against Israel as juxtaposed to the nature of Israel's calling as God's People. Verse 1 begins with the Qal plural imperative of the verb *shāmaʿ* that denotes "to hear."[125] What the Israelites are commanded to hear is "this message." The particular message that Yahweh is instructing them to hear is further emphasized with the demonstrative pronoun "this." Yahweh wants them both "to hear" and "to obey" this message given by Amos. The *shāmaʿ* denotes both "to hear" and "to obey." The message which is spoken against the nation of Israel illustrates that the Lord is in an adversarial role with them due to their misdeeds. They are addressed as the "Sons of Israel" and the "entire clan" with whom the Lord has an endearing and extended relationship.[126] Yahweh is described as the one who brought Israel up from Egypt. The book of Amos generally, and Amos 3:1 and

2 more specifically, assume a relationship of Yahweh with Israel that is predicated upon the past history of deliverance that is referenced in this immediate passage.

The recollection of this event assumes the historicity of the Exodus event. Even if one questions the historicity of the Exodus event, one must at least conclude that from the vantage point of Amos and his audience, the Exodus is considered to be a historical event. This personal history between Yahweh and Israel is also emphasized in verse 2 with the grammatical phrase "you only." The phrase "you only" is in an emphatic position ahead of the verb, contrary to normal Hebrew sentence word order. "You only" means "you alone," or "you and no one else." The verb translated "chosen" (*yāda ʾtî*) is the word "to know" and suggests an intimate relationship between God and his people. As such, the phrase "only you alone have I known" implies the "elect" status of Israel and the special nature of their calling. The Lord has selected Israel and this election goes back to the call of Abram. The special status of Israel as the "Elect of the Lord" leads to increased accountability.[127] The breaking of the covenant responsibilities leads to divine punishment by the Lord Himself. Amos uses special language to describe the intimate relationship between Yahweh and Israel. Moreover, Amos uses special language to describe the ensuing punishment that is to be meted out by Yahweh Himself. The latter part of Amos 3:2 states the Lord's actions are consequences of their misdeeds. The Lord will "visit" Israel for all of the sins that have been committed. The word "visit" is also present in Amos 3:14:

> "On the day I punish Israel for her sins, I will destroy the altars of Bethel; the horns of the altar will be cut off and fall to the ground."

The term "to visit" is found 304 times in the Hebrew Bible. *Pāqad* is used in Genesis 21:1 to describe the intervention of Yahweh in the fulfillment of the promise to Sarah and to Hannah (1 Sam 2:21). Yahweh's promise to both women was the birth of a child while they were still in their state of barrenness. There is also a military nuance of the use of *pāqad*, which the writer suggests reflects the metaphor Yahweh as a warrior. This use reflects the "grace in reverse" theme that one sees in the curses and blessings of Deuteronomy 28 and Leviticus 26. The curses are a reversal of direct intervention of the Lord to care for, sustain, and prosper the nation of Israel. Furthermore, there is imagery in the Old Testament of Yahweh as a warrior. The Lord is depicted as a warrior who fights for Israel (Exodus 15:3).[128] In the Song of the Sea, Yahweh is celebrated as a "Man of War" for his exploits against Egypt in the plagues. The imagery of Yahweh as a warrior displays the fact that Yahweh will fight
against the enemies of Israel and in the same vein fight against Israel when they violate the covenant relationship with Yahweh.[129]

2. Amos 7:7-9

7:7 "He showed me this: I saw the sovereign One standing by a tin wall holding tin in his hand.

7:8 The Lord said to me, 'What do you see, Amos?' I said, 'Tin.' The Sovereign One then said, 'Look, I am about to place tin among my people Israel. I will no longer overlook their sin.'

7:9 Isaac's centers of worship will become desolate; Israel's holy places will be in ruins. I will attack Jeroboam's dynasty with the sword.'"

Amos 7:7-9 is the third of five visions in Amos found in Amos 7:1-9:15. The third vision deals with the Lord in judgment against Israel. The image used here in this passage has traditionally been translated as that of the Lord judging Israel though the image of a "plumb line." The writer suggests that the image here is not that of a "plumb line" but rather that of a "tin wall" or a "lead wall." The development of this idea in mentioned by Niehaus and Stuart in their commentaries on Amos.[130] The word ʾănāk is an Akkadian word that is used to denote tin or lead. As such, the specific use of the "Akkadian" may function as a veiled reference to the impending armies and destruction of Israel by the Assyrians. The term ʾănāk or "tin" can point to the multivalent use of this vision with the overall meaning still being that of the destruction of the nation by the incoming Assyrian army. However, the full development and the discussion of this idea is beyond the scope of this paper.

In verse 8, one sees imagery that is connected with the Exodus. In verses 8 and 9, Yahweh states that he will "no longer overlook their sin" and that the holy places of Israel will be reduced to ruins. The language of the later part of verse makes reference to the final plague of the death of the firstborn. One sees the mention of this in Exodus 12:12 and 23:

12:12 "On that same night I will pass through Egypt and strike down every firstborn of both people and animals, and I will bring judgment on all the gods of Egypt, I am the LORD.

12:23 When the LORD goes through the land to strike down the Egyptians, He will see the blood on the top and sides of the doorframe and will pass over that doorway, and he will not permit the destroyer to enter your houses and strike you down."

The verb *'ābar* is used to denote "to cross" or "to pass over." As such *'ābar* describes the actions of the Death Angel. When He sees the blood of a lamb splattered on the doorframe he would "pass over" and not strike anyone in the house of the Israelites. The specific use of this verb is a clear reference to the Tenth Plague of the Exodus. Additionally, Stuart links this use of Amos 7:9 to covenant curses mentioned in Leviticus 26:30-31. In Leviticus 26:30-31, one finds the following:

26:30. "I will destroy your high places and cut down your incense altars, and I will stack your dead bodies on top of the lifeless bodies of your idols. I will abhor you.

26:31 I will lay your cities waste and make your sanctuaries desolate, and I will refuse to smell your soothing aromas."

Stuart compiles a list of covenant curses and a list of covenant blessings that one finds in the Torah, specifically the books of Leviticus and Deuteronomy. Stuart compiles a list of blessings consisting of 27 categories of covenant curses that one finds in the Pentateuch.[131] The list of blessings consists of 10 individual types of benefits that the Lord will administer for covenant obedience. According to Stuart, Amos 7:9 should be categorized as Curse Types 9a and 18.

The devastation of the sanctuaries as mentioned, curse type 9a, in Leviticus 26:31 and Amos 7:9 share the terms "be destroyed," "high places," and "sanctuary." Additionally, one notes the destruction of the royalty.[132] For Stuart, this is curse type 18 and it involves the loss of family as is stated in Deuteronomy 32:25. The threat to the family of Jeroboam is mentioned in the latter part of Amos 7:9, which states "I will attack Jeroboam's dynasty with the sword." The "sword," metonymy, for violent death is mentioned both in Deuteronomy 32:25 and in general, the "sword," is punishment that is indicative of covenant infidelity.

3. Amos 8:8-10

8:8 "Because of this the earth will quake, and all who live in it will mourn.

The whole earth will rise like the River Nile, it will surge upward and then grow calm, like the Nile in Egypt.

8:9 'In that day,' says the sovereign LORD, 'I will make the sun set at noon, and make the earth dark in the middle of the day.

8:10 I will turn your festivals into funerals, and all your songs into funeral dirges.

I will make everyone wear funeral clothes and cause every head to be shaved bald. I will make you mourn as if you had lost your only son; when it ends it will indeed have been a bitter day.'"

Amos 8:8-10 is a portion of Amos 8:4-14 that consists of an oracle that follows the fourth vision of Amos (8:1-3). This material appended to the fourth vision consists of three short paragraphs (8:8-10).¹³³ This section answers the question regarding the significance of the fourth vision. The overall idea in this section is that Yahweh's intervention will bring wailing and there will be no word from Yahweh. Amos 8:8-10 states that mourning will take place on the day of divine judgement. There are two themes in this section. One, God will judge the land. Two, the people of Israel will mourn. The judgment of the land is likened to the flooding of the Nile River. In this oracle in verses 4-6, the immediate wrong actions are financial abuses of the needy. This is the reason that the Lord will act in judgment. In verse 8 there is judgment by earthquake.¹³⁴ In verse 8 the earth will quake and the inhabitants will mourn, not only for the quaking of the land, but for the dead.

An earthquake is a familiar portent of the anger of the Lord. An earthquake is expressed by the verb *ragaz*, which denotes "to tremble." The earthquake is a dominant motif of judgment in Amos (2:13; 314-15; 9:1). Moreover, the dating of the book is assisted by the mention of the call of Amos and his prophetic activity in the context of the reign of King Uzziah in Judah and King Jeroboam in Israel, two years before the earthquake.¹³⁵ This terrestrial upheaval with all its concomitant destruction and tragedy shall result in the mourning of the entire population.¹³⁶ The death and destruction in verse 8 are curses that have been prophesied for covenant disloyalty.

For Stuart, the description of the calamities in verse 8 are Curse Type 25.¹³⁷ The rising and falling of the Nile were a well-known annual occurrence. Egyptian agriculture relied heavily on the annual flooding of the Nile. The waters flooded in September and receded in October, leaving a short winter period for cultivation of crops. Occasionally the flood was too weak, with catastrophic results, and Egyptian texts often note "a year of low Nile" with hunger and misery.

In Amos 8:9 and 10, there is judgment by solar eclipse. In verse 9, the description of the sun setting at noon is classic prophetic language dealing with divine intervention. Two such eclipses have been calculated to have occurred during the time of Amos. They occurred in 784 and 763 BCE. The eclipse is directly a result of divine intervention and is a component of the vocabulary of the Day of the Lord (5:18, 20). Eclipses were considered to be as result of the anger of the Lord. This was also true of the larger Ancient Near East. The darkness of the day of divine judgment is reminiscent of the ninth Plague against Egypt in which there was darkness for three days. One can see the clear typology of the ninth Plague of Darkness and the tenth Plague of Death of the firstborn, with the events concerning the Crucifixion of Jesus with the concomitant astrological occurrences. In verse 10, Bethel Temple festivals and joyous songs will be transformed into wailing and lamenting when God judges Israel "in that day." The customary signs of mourning will be everywhere as people put on sackcloth, shave, and pull out their hair. The people will mourn as deeply as one weeping uncontrollably over the death of an only son.

The mention of the mourning for an only son is again a clear reference to the last plague in which the Death Angel kills the first born of all in the land of Egypt, except for the people of Israel.

4. Amos 9:7-8

9:7 "Are not you Israelites the same to me as the Cushites?" declares the LORD. 'Did I not bring Israel up from Egypt, the Philistines from Caphtor and the Arameans from Kir?'

9:8 'Surely the eyes of the Sovereign LORD are on the sinful kingdom. I will destroy it from the face of the earth. Yet I will not totally destroy the descendants of Jacob,' declares the LORD."

Amos 9:7-8 is a part of the dispute found in the larger context of Amos 9:7-10. The vision cycle off Amos 7-9 is completed by the fifth vision found in Amos 9:1-4 and a hymn in Amos 9:5-6. The dispute in Amos 9:7-10 begins with two rhetorical questions in Amos 9:7. The first compares the Israelites to Cushites. The reason for choosing the Cushites is unclear. The Nubians, or Cushites, were Black tribes in Africa south of the second cataract of the Nile.[138] In this regard, does the reference signify that they are a relatively obscure people and when compared to the Israelites there is the argument of the lesser to the greater in terms of the discussion?[139] Perhaps they were despised as one might surmise by the attack on Moses by Miriam and Aaron as narrated in Numbers 12. If the Israelites are like the Cushites, the idea may be that Israelites are no different than the Cushites and have no special privileges before the Lord. In the same vein, this idea of relocation is referenced with respect to the Israelites. In verse 7, the mention of the Children of Israel being delivered from Egypt is noted. The use of the verb *'lh* to denote "to go up" or "ascend" to describe the Exodus is important.[140] The use in the *hiphil* in Hebrew clearly points to the divine activity of the Lord on behalf of Israel.[141]

The second rhetorical question of Amos 7:9 compares God's mighty deliverance of the people of God with His bringing the Philistines from Captor and the Syrians from Kir. In these events, one sees that the sovereignty of God that is assumed in the book of Amos and clearly displayed in the judgment oracles of Amos 1 and 2.[142] In verse 8, Amos affirms that the Lord will bring judgment on Israel. Amos emphatically affirms that Yahweh will destroy the sinful nation of Israel from the face of the earth. The use of the term *shāmad* that denotes "to destroy" is suggestive of the covenantal curses that the Lord will bring upon Israel as a consequence for disobedience. One sees the connection of disobedience and destruction described in Amos echoed in Leviticus 26:30:

> "I will destroy your high places, cut down your incense altars and pile your dead bodies on the lifeless forms of your idols, and I will abhor you."

The use of the term in this verse is instructive. *Shāmad* is an important term used in the book of Joshua. In Joshua, *shāmad* describes the activity of God and the use of this term is a reference to the destruction of foreign nations during the Conquest by Joshua.[143] In a significant portion of the uses of *shāmad*, the basic meaning of the term suggests the wholesale destruction of a group of people. In non-theological texts, *shāmad* refers to the destruction of a family (Gen. 34:30), a national group (2 Sam. 21:5; Esth. 3:6, 13), or many nations (Isa. 10:7). Rarely does it refer to the killing of a single person (2 Sam. 14:7, 11, 16). Nearly four-fifths of the occurrences of שׁמד carry a heavy theological load since they are in contexts where

God is the immediate or implied subject. Extermination comes upon a nation or class of people because they have fallen under the judgment of God. Two-thirds of the theological uses occur in Deuteronomy or Deuteronomistic texts (Joshua through 2 Kings). The Old Testament authors have appropriated the word as indicating what God will do or did to the nations that inhabited the land of Canaan. Deuteronomy 7:23–24 is typical:

> "But the LORD your God will deliver them over to you, throwing them into great confusion until they are destroyed. He will give their kings into your hand, and you will wipe out their names from under heaven. No one will be able to stand up against you; you will destroy them."

This was a part of the theology of the gift of the land. The inhabitants had to be annihilated because of their abominations, lest Israel learn their ways and abandon God.[144] The destruction depicted by *shāmad* usually involves a rather sudden catastrophe such as warfare or a mass killing, but in one passage it is the result of attrition due to famine and oppression (Deut. 28:48, 63). In yet another passage God is depicted as the basic cause of the destruction, while his people are His instruments of destruction. The book of Joshua exhibits a theme that is developed in Exodus which is God as a warrior. This is a prominent theme in the Old Testament and particularly in the book of Exodus. The use of *shāmad* shows that the nation of Israel is an object of divine wrath. What God did in the Conquest to the 31 conquered city-states of Canaan, He will now inflict upon His covenant people.

5. Amos 5: 8

5: 8 "But there is one who made the constellations Pleiades and Orion; he can turn the darkness into morning, and daylight into night.

He summons the water of the seas and pours it out on the earth's surface. The LORD is his name!"

The mention of astrological language in this hymn celebrates Yahweh's control and governance over nature. Yahweh makes the constellations and controls the alteration of night into day. The mention of the seas may be a reference to the original act of creation in Genesis 1. There is the theme of de-creation in the Plagues of Egypt. The mention of turning darkness into morning and daylight into night can be a reference to the Plague of Darkness in Exodus 10:21- 23.

6. Amos 5:12

5:12 "Certainly I am aware of your many rebellious acts and your numerous sins. You torment the innocent, you take bribes, and you deny justice to the needy at the city gate."

Amos 5:12 is located within a larger lament against the nation of Israel that is located in Amos 5:1-17. Amos 5:12 notes that the Lord is cognizant of the rebellious acts of leading citizens of Israel. The denial of justice for the needy and the abuse of the poor is clearly prohibited in the Covenant Code of Exodus 20:19-23:33. On this verse, Stuart states the following:

> Consciously, purposely, Israelite leading citizens were persecuting the righteous (or "innocent " or *ṣaddîq*) by taking bribe money either for declaring poor peoples' cases against the rich to be without merit, or by ruling in favor of rich plaintiffs or defendants against poor plaintiffs or defendants (cf. Exod. 23:6–8; 1 Sam. 12:3; Isa. 10:2; 29:21; Mal. 3:5). Such a direct covenant violation (cf. Exod. 23:1–8; Deut. 16:18–20) is heinous.[145]

Amos 5:12 addresses the wickedness of the legal system. The topic of false justice begins in verse 7. The lament in verse 12 attacks the criminals and sinners. The Lord knows who they are and that His laws have been broken. Amos 5:12 assumes the importance of the Covenant Code for the nation and there is the assumption that this code of economic and social behavior was deemed the appropriate code of conduct. The Covenant Code details the normal life of the community and what was to be expected in their interactions with each other as the Lord's Chosen People. The Covenant Code covered all the essential areas of life including devotion to God, commitment to personal integrity and morality, family responsibilities, judicial principles, and national days of worship.[146] Violation of the Covenant Code was a violation of the status as God's Chosen People and the ethics that were demanded in the Torah. In Amos, there is a violation of the Covenant Code and syncretism (or idolatry) with the two worship centers of Bethel and Dan for the Northern Kingdom. One also notes that in Exodus, both the Covenant Code and the Golden Calf incident are literarily and chronological in immediate proximity. In this regard, Amos connects economic injustice with idolatry. Thus, God's vision for His People includes orthodox worship and justice for the marginalized—the Gospelist tradition of Black Christians in the modern world is consistent with biblical tradition.

Reuse of Scripture and Tradition by Amos: Some Preliminary Conclusions

In this survey of some of the terminology used by Amos taken from the book of Exodus, three of them reference the Plagues against Egypt. Two of the passages refer to the Exodus itself. One passage refers to the Covenant Code of Exodus 20-23. This is a partial list of the passages that reference the Exodus and other important events and persons that comprise the rich tradition of God's engagement with Israel. The following list are some conclusions based on the passages that I have examined and Amos' use of historical traditions in general.

1. References to the Exodus, the Plagues against Egypt, and the Conquest of Canaan that point to the social, economic, and ethical responsibilities of God's grace. God's Chosen People were expected to act in a certain manner. This manner was described in detail in the Law of the Lord. Violations of the covenant would lead to curses from the Lord.
2. The referencing of the Exodus, the Plagues upon Egypt, and the Conquest point to the historicity of these events. If one argues about the historicity of these events, one has to at least acknowledge that from the vantage point of Amos and his audience, these events were considered to be historical events.
3. There is an assumption that the People of God define themselves by the intervention of Yahweh on their behalf,

even if the intervention is to inflict punishment due to covenant disloyalty.

4. The deliverance of Israel from Egypt, God's election of them, and the giving of the law were the bases for their ethical actions towards each other as a nation and governed their interactions with their neighbors.
5. The use of Exodus and Conquest motifs in the context of an impending invasion by Assyria and the subsequent exile function as grace in reverse. It is ironic in that the same language used to describe the Exodus, the Conquest, and their status as God's Elect is now used in an opposite context. The context is one of judgment, death, and exile.
6. Exodus highlights the theme in the Bible of God as a Warrior. In Exodus, God is a warrior for the people of God in their struggle for liberation. In Amos, God is a warrior against Israel as a result of their covenant disloyalty. The reuse of the theme of God as a warrior is emphasized in Amos 1 and 2 by the presence of war oracles and the implementation of covenantal curses.
7. The framework of Deuteronomy is that of a vassal treaty with blessings and curses for adherence and violation of the covenant agreement. This framework of the book of Deuteronomy as a second millennium biblical document helps to support the idea of the antiquity of the book of Deuteronomy in this time period. The location of Deuteronomy in this time period supports the issue of Mosaic authority and also is in sharp contrast to the Documentary Hypothesis, which classifies Deuteronomy as a D-document with a sixth century BCE date. The utilization of the curses of Deuteronomy in the book of Amos, which is an eighth-century document, also

supports the traditional fifteenth century BCE date of the book of Deuteronomy.
8. The framework of Leviticus with blessings and curses for adherence and non- adherence to the covenant between Yahweh and the nation of Israel also contains elements of a suzerainty treaty. As such, the date of authorship of Leviticus is also during the fifteenth century BCE, which is the date for the traditional figure of Moses.

The use of re-contextualization of the curses of Leviticus 26 in the book of Amos, an eighth-century document, additionally helps to support the antiquity of the book of Leviticus as a fifteenth-century document. The use of the curses in Leviticus 26 as noted by Stuart supports the idea that the book of Leviticus was an existing document that was contextually re-applied by Amos. This perspective is in strong disagreement with the Documentary Hypothesis, which suggests that Leviticus is a sixth-century literary creation, the P-document, created by an exilic priestly community.

Reuse of Scripture and Tradition by Amos: My Assumptions About Amos and Reflections as a Gospelist Scholar

1. When I examine the book of Amos, what becomes more confirmed and apparent to me is the following: there is an obvious inadequacy of the term "evangelical" in the experience of people of color. For myself as a scholar of color, there are social, spiritual, and economic implications of our relationship with the Lord. To ignore the ethical, economic, and social implications of the gospel for the

sake of a narrow definition of "spirituality" is to miss the message of the Gospel of Jesus Christ.

2. I was not prepared for the racism of my seminary experience and experiences dealing within the European-American evangelical community. One of my graduate school classmates helped me to understand and deal with the inconsistency of this high view of scripture and a "low view" of people of color.

3. My methodology of hermeneutics is to look at the text from a grammatical-historical viewpoint. This viewpoint involves a high view of Scripture. I am comfortable with the word "inerrancy" when used to describe the original documents. When I examine the prophets and the teachings of Jesus, it is clear that there are ethical, social, and justice motifs that are addressed in and important to the Bible.

4. A methodology that does not deal with class, race, and economics is not exegetical.

5. As I see it, one cannot omit race, class, gender, and economics from the biblical text.

6. The moral imperative of the book of Amos keeps the message of the Old Testament from being spiritualized.

7. The advent of Jesus in John 1:1-18 utilizes language of the Exodus event and in my thinking, keeps one from over-spiritualizing the message of the Cross.

8. African-Americans have re-contextualized the Old Testament narratives in general and the Exodus in particular to deal with the long history of slavery and abuse in the United States and beyond—a tradition we here call Gospel Haymanot. The story of the Exodus is powerful and gave people of color who were enslaved

hope. The hope is that God can deliver and does deliver from any and every difficulty. The hope and confidence is that deliverance is only a prayer away. The religious history, culture, and music of African-Americans is "soaked" with the message of hope and the language of deliverance that one finds in God's Word.

9. The God of the Bible re-contextualizes Himself for His Covenant People. As such the Bible is a timeless message of hope, deliverance, and liberation for all.

BIBLIOGRAPHY

Brown, F, Driver, S., Briggs, C. *The Brown-Driver-Briggs Hebrew and English Lexicon: With an Appendix Containing the Aramaic Coded with the Numbering System from Strong's Exhaustive Concordance of the Bible*. Peabody, MA: Hendrickson, Publishers, 1996.

Garrett, Duane A. *A Commentary on Exodus*. Grand Rapids, MI: Kregel Publications, 2014.

Hall, Gary H. "דָּם‎". In *New International Dictionary of Old Testament Theology and Exegesis*, Vol. 4. Grand Rapids, MI: Zondervan Academic, 2012.

Hubbard, David Allan. *Tyndale Old Testament Commentaries: Joel and Amos*. Downers Grove, IL: InterVarsity Press, 1990.

Longman III Tremper and Daniel G. Reid, *God is a Warrior*. Grand Rapids, MI: Zondervan Publishing, 1995.

Niehaus, Jeffrey. "Amos." In *The Minor Prophets: An Exegetical and Expository Commentary*, edited by Thomas Edward McComiskey. Grand Rapids, MI: Baker Book House, 1992.

Robertson, Cleotha. "Amos." In *The Africana Bible: Reading Israel's Scriptures from Africa and the African Diaspora*, edited by Hugh R. Page, Jr., Minneapolis, MN: Fortress Press, 2010.

Smith, Gary V. *The NIV Application Commentary: Hosea, Amos, Micah*. Grand Rapids, MI: Zondervan, 2001.

———. "Continuity and Discontinuity in Amos' Use of Tradition." *The Journal of the Evangelical Theological Society* 34.1 (1991)

Stuart, Douglas. *Word Biblical Commentary: Hosea-Jonah*, Vol. 31. Grand Rapids, MI: Zondervan, 1988.

3

WORTHY OF THE GOSPEL:
Aliens, Slaves, and Women as Our Teachers

DENNIS R. EDWARDS

Introduction

Perhaps it is human nature to take our behavioral cues from society's elite. Our role models and influencers tend to be wealthy, beautiful, well-connected, and even egotistical. The tendency to bypass virtuous but unimpressive individuals while pursuing the popular and prideful is present in the Christian community as well as the larger society. But the NT stresses that those on the margins of society, those least impressive in the eyes of the world, are the people who most resemble the Lord Jesus Christ. Because of their resemblance to the Lord, those most likely to be overlooked may actually be our best teachers of spiritual truth.

Mystic, poet, and theologian Howard Thurman, in *Jesus and the Disinherited*, mused on the alienation Jesus of Nazareth—and many of his followers—must have experienced as non-citizens of the Roman Empire. "In essence, Rome was the enemy; Rome symbolized total frustration; Rome was the great barrier to peace of mind. And Rome was everywhere. No Jewish person of the period could deal with the question of his practical life, his vocation, his place in society, until first he had settled deep within himself this critical issue. This is the position of the disinherited in every age."[147] Thurman sought to encourage "those whose backs are against the wall" to have Jesus of Nazareth, a poor, non-citizen Jew, serve as the ultimate role model. In this volume, Vince Bantu advances the idea of Gospel Haymanot, which combines the notions of orthodoxy (right thinking about faith in Jesus Christ), and orthopraxis (right practice of the faith) by black and brown people, who are among the most marginalized in our world.

This essay examines the notion of citizenship (and non-citizenship) with Gospel Haymanot principles in view. Philippians and 1 Peter point us to conclude that those of lower status in the Roman Empire: aliens, slaves, and women, are among our best teachers of what it means to be worthy of the gospel of Jesus Christ. By extension of that notion, Christians on the margins of contemporary society may also serve as prime exemplars of Christian faith.

Citizenship Has Its Privileges

A brief passage, Acts 16:35-40, recounts the release of the apostle Paul and Silas from a prison in Philippi. The two evangelists were invited to "go in peace." But Paul objects, saying, "They have beaten us in public, uncondemned, men who are Roman citizens, and have thrown us into prison; and now are they going to discharge us in secret? Certainly not! Let them come and take us out themselves." Paul is able to challenge the authorities on the basis of his and Silas' status as citizens of Rome, and it is their citizenship that provokes fear among the magistrates. Earlier in Acts 16, in Luke's recounting of the evangelization of Philippi, he notes that Philippi was, "a leading [*prōtos*] city of the district of Macedonia and a Roman colony" (16:12). With this information, Luke prepares readers for the aforementioned encounter, where Roman citizenship allows Paul to advocate, at least to some degree, for Silas and himself.

Roman imperialism appears to be in the background of Paul's association with the Philippians in both Acts as well as Paul's letter to the Philippians. In my published article, "Good Citizenship: A Study of Philippians 1:27 and its Implications for Contemporary Urban Ministry," I assert that at various points in his letter, the apostle Paul is deliberately invoking the concept of citizenship in the Greco-Roman world.[148] Lynn Cohick, debating Paul's engagement with Roman imperialism in her treatment of Philippians and Empire, observes that "Paul uses explicitly civic or political terms in Philippians 1:27 (*polituesthe*) and Philippians 3:20 (*politeuma*), and describes Jesus as Savior, an unusual term for Paul, but more commonly found describing the emperor or victorious general."[149]

The title of this paper, "Worthy of the Gospel," is derived from Phil 1:27, but I will focus more on the letter of 1 Peter. However, I bring up Philippi and Paul's connection to it by way of contrast. Our understanding of Paul's engagement with Philippi, in person as well as in writing, is enhanced by our appreciation of Roman citizenship. Paul's suffering for the sake of the gospel is all the more pathetic when our picture of Paul is that of someone with relative privilege due to his status as a citizen, yet is treated unfairly. Paul is the messenger of Jesus who speaks to kings (see

Acts 9:15) and is even emboldened to evangelize the Praetorian Guard during his imprisonment. Cohick points out that the Praetorian Guard "had power," yet, "Paul, apparently, was not intimidated by that power."[150]

On the one hand, there is the story of Paul and the Philippians. That story invites us to reflect on the propagation of the gospel of Jesus within a Roman colony populated by Roman farmers and military veterans, those who might be counted among the most patriotic.[151] On the other hand, there are the Christians addressed in the letter called 1 Peter. First Peter, according to Miroslav Volf, is "the epistle whose main theme is Christian life in a non-Christian environment," and "the one text which speaks more pointedly and comprehensively to the problem of 'Christ and culture' than any other in the NT."[152]

"Citizens worthy of the gospel" are not only those who can appeal to their status as citizens of the secular society, but must also include those who have been pushed to the margins of that secular society, perhaps even with no claim as citizens. For them, being members of God's household (see 1 Pet 2:9-10) is the main identity marker and these marginalized Christians serve as teachers for subsequent generations who may be intimidated by the power of the empire. First Peter demonstrates that marginalized Christians—those without citizenship in the secular society, or who are second-class citizens—are nevertheless among our best guides as to what it means to be followers of Jesus.

The Model Citizen

There is speculation that Erastus, mentioned in Rom 16:23 as the city treasurer (*ho oikonomos tēs poleōs*), is the same Erastus commended in a Latin inscription found in Corinth: "Erastus laid this pavement at his own expense, in appreciation of his appointment as aedile."¹⁵³ Even if these writings refer to different men, the point is that working for the common good was one way of gaining honor. As many scholars have noted, honor was of supreme value in the First-Century. Honor was reckoned by the currency of one's good name, fame, esteem from others, and also social ranking.¹⁵⁴ Citizens were in the best position to give and receive honor.

Mary Beard asserts that, "[Roman] citizenship brought with it all kinds of specific rights under Roman law, covering a wide range of topics, from contracts to punishments. The simple reason that, in the 60s CE, Saint Peter was crucified while Saint Paul enjoyed the privilege of being beheaded was that Paul was a Roman citizen."¹⁵⁵ When I noted that citizenship held privileges I was not thinking of a quick death versus a slow one, but we should get the point that citizenship meant advantage in a variety of ways. Model citizens were those who gained honor, at times through their beneficence. For Roman citizens, however, honor was not always associated with morality, as our understanding of Roman sexual behavior might lead us to surmise. Even today, it seems that some Christians are more impressed by those who have power and prominence in society, i.e., honor, even if lacking in morals. Barth Campbell observes, "The pivotal value in first-century Mediterranean society is honor...Honor is a claim to worth and the social acknowledgement publicly that her/his actions conform to social obligations."¹⁵⁶ As John Elliott concludes, in 1 Peter "honor ultimately is ascribed not according to blood and birth, as convention would dictate, nor is it achieved by one heroic act of valor and *andreia* ("manliness," "courage"). Instead it is conferred by an act of divine grace, by the favor of a God who gives grace to the lowly (5:5); a divine patron who raises slaves to the status of sons and daughters (2:18-15) and wives to the status of coheirs of the grace of life (3:1-7)."[157]

I want to stress that not only are we to laud the Christians who first read 1 Peter, we should see them as teachers. And by extension, we still find teachers among those who are dishonored in society because they lack social status tied to citizenship. Despite that marginal status—rather *because* of such status—Christians who are non-citizens and second-class citizens often embody the values and virtues of Jesus in a way that the dominant culture might not. For example, marginalized believers in the USA, such as immigrants, African Americans and other diaspora Christians, women, and disabled people, demonstrate the power of Christian faith to face injustice.[158] In other words, the Gospel Haymanot values are powerfully present among the marginalized.

Aliens Who Changed the World

There is no shortage of studies or debate surrounding the terms 1 Peter uses in describing the readers, particularly *eklektos*, *parepidēmos*, *diaspora*, and *paroikia*, and not enough space presently to examine all the data. However, the commentaries discuss the degree to which these descriptions should be taken literally or metaphorically. I agree with the assessment of Steven R. Bechtler that the terms "are figures of speech, metaphors, by which a situation of social alienness is characterized."[159] While all four of those aforementioned words are important in understanding the social situation of Peter's readers, I only want to focus on the two that occur together in 1 Pet 2:11, *paroikia* and *parepidēmos*, translated as "aliens" and "exiles" in the NRSV.

Elliott takes "aliens" and "exiles" to have a literal, geographic significance, indicating those who have made their homes in places other than that of their ancestors through immigration—forced as well as voluntary.[160] Yet, the Christians are not aliens and exiles merely in a spiritual sense, as if to say that their true home is heaven and they are foreigners on earth.[161] The terms *paroikia* and *parepidēmos*, occur in Gen 23:4 (LXX) where Abraham describes his situation among the Hittites. Bechtler asserts, "First Peter urges certain kinds of behavior upon its readers as people in a socially liminal position analogous to that of Abraham."[162]

That is to say that Peter's emphasis is on the social and cultural distance between the Christian community and their unredeemed neighbors. It is because of their faith in Jesus Christ that Peter's audience is foreign to those around them. Foreigners in Peter's time, and arguably in our own as well, are often held at arm's length, so to speak, as they are typically viewed with suspicion and have an unstable position within the dominant culture. Also, a stranger or foreigner is not expected to know or participate in the customs of the host culture. Such was the case with Peter's audience (see 1:13-21). "The moral estrangement Christians experienced in their society was a consequence of not sharing society's values and customs."[163] The audience of 1 Peter was functionally, even if perhaps not literally, non-citizens. Yet, as non-citizens they are called upon to be witnesses of the new birth (see 1:3) through their morally upright behavior as well as their respect for civil authority.

Perhaps the most famous example of the disdain some had for Christianity is found in a letter from Pliny the Younger to Trajan. Trajan was the emperor of Rome and Pliny the Younger was governor of Pontus and Bithynia from 111-113 CE. Pliny likely writes a few years after the time of 1 Peter, and governed a region where some of the recipients of 1 Peter lived (see 1 Pet 1:1). In his letter, Pliny describes his practice of interrogation and persecution of Christians.[164] Despite the contempt that Roman citizens may have had for the Christians, First Peter alleges that the Christian's good conduct—something not common among the pagans (literally "nations" or "Gentiles")—might find approval among unbelievers. It turns out that within the decadent ancient Greco-Roman society, some Gentiles demonstrated an understanding of what might be considered upright behavior. Stephen C. Barton writes that, "the moral rigor that attracted pagans to Christianity and Judaism was not without parallel in Greco-Roman society beyond the church and synagogue. It needs to be recognized more widely that many pagans converted to Christianity because they found in the Christian groups moral standards that they recognized already as profoundly important for human welfare".[165] Apparently, some among the pagans found aspects of Christian ethics and morality alluring.

In 1 Pet 2:16, the aliens and strangers of 1 Peter are given the paradoxical encouragement to live as free slaves. Directly following that admonition are the author's instructions for household servants (*oiketai*). Slaves who follow Jesus become models for all Christians. "Regardless of one's social status, Christians are to consider themselves to be slaves to God, and so the actual slave who is obedient to his master exemplifies that role for the entire Christian community."[166]

Slaves: Suffering Revolutionaries

Slaves had minimal social status in Ancient Rome. As Achtemeier puts it, slaves were "defined as chattel who, lacking citizenship, lacked the essential qualification of humanity."[167] In 2:18 the author addresses household slaves with the command to submit to their masters "in all fear" (literally).[168] The same attitude that the entire community should have toward God (1:17; 2:17) must be expressly evident among slaves toward their masters. J. Ramsey Michaels notes well that in v. 18, "Although the word order could suggest that the reverence is directed toward slave masters…the clear distinction in 2:17 between reverence toward God and respect for the emperor demands that here too fo/boß means reverence toward God and not human masters."[169]

Godly slaves must submit to their masters no matter how kind or harsh the treatment from those masters might be, and the emphasis is on the latter situation. This dimension of 1 Peter's command is especially difficult to hear with my 21st-century ears.

It must be seen, however, that 1 Peter gives absolutely no validation of harsh treatment by slave masters; 2:19 makes explicit that the slaves' suffering is unjust. First Peter's advocacy of non-retaliatory behavior is not an endorsement of slavery, and is also not an indication of the weakness of slaves. Peaceful submission to even the harshest of masters is evidence of genuine Christian faith. The point is to grasp what Christ-like behavior looks like in one of the most difficult situations imaginable. Slaves, though in a horrible, unenviable position, have the peculiar honor of serving as living examples of what Jesus is like. The slaves model what is important to God.

The early Christians—especially slaves—were not in the position to overturn Roman society's oppressive and hierarchical social structure. However, as Volf contends, "the call to follow the crucified Messiah was, in the long run, much more effective in changing the unjust political, economic, and familial structures than direct exhortations to revolutionize them would ever have been. For an allegiance to the crucified Messiah—indeed, worship of a crucified God—is an eminently political act that subverts a politics of dominion at its core."[170] Volf proceeds with the following recommendation:

> What we should learn from the text [1 Peter] is not, of course, to keep our mouths shut and hands folded, but to make our rhetoric and action more modest so that they can be more effective. As we strive for social change, 1 Peter nudges us to drop the pen that scripts master narratives and instead give account of the living hope in God and God's future (3:15; 1:5), to abandon the project of reshaping society from the ground up and instead do as much as we can from where we are at the time we are there (2:11), to suffer injustice and bless the unjust rather than perpetrating violence by repaying 'evil for evil or abuse for abuse' (3:9), and to replace the anger of frustration with the joy of expectation (4:13).[171]

Volf's admonition might find an easier reception among the dominant culture, but even as a person of color, I find a measure of hope that allegiance to Christ can be a subversive act within a culture that depends upon violence and intimidation in order to maintain social order.

Social order in Ancient Rome required women to be subordinate to men. Therefore, while women could be citizens of Rome, their status was inferior to that of men; women were second-class citizens. Yet, from their lowly status, we learn the power of wordless witness, which is to say that when it comes to advancing the gospel, actions might speak louder than words (1 Pet 3:1).

Women: Silent Evangelists

Beard relays a mid second-century epitaph commemorating a woman named Claudia: "Here is the unlovely grave of a lovely woman. She loved her husband with her heart. She bore two sons. One of these she leaves on earth, the other under the earth. She was graceful in her speech and elegant in her step. She kept the home. She made wool. That is what there is to say."[172] Even though this tribute to Claudia is well before the time of 1 Peter, it reflects a social status of women that did not change much for many years. During the first century women could not vote or hold office, could not testify in court, and could not be the legal guardian of their own children. Plutarch advocated for a degree of mutuality in marriage, suggesting, for example, that husbands and wives hold material possessions in common. However, Plutarch maintained the superiority of husbands, with husbands determining which gods the family would worship—something relevant to 1 Pet 3:1-6.[173]

According to 1 Pet 3:1, wives, just like the household slaves, are to take their behavioral cues from the Lord Jesus. It would be wrong to understand 1 Peter as suggesting any natural inferiority of women to men (v. 7 notwithstanding). 1 Peter does not suggest or require that all women be submissive to all men. In fact, wives are instructed explicitly to submit to their "own" (*idios*) husbands. This is not to say that 1 Peter has 21st-century sensibilities in mind, but rather to say that the author's interest is particularly with the household unit. Wives can do their part to minimize conflict by adopting a Christ-like posture toward their husbands. In fact, such humble behavior may have the power to win over their non-Christian husbands.

To say that husbands "may be won over" (*kerdainō*) stresses the persuasive element involved in evangelism. It is the same way the apostle Paul speaks of communicating the Good News in 1 Cor 9:19-22 (where the word occurs some five times). In a similar way that Paul offers his strategy for winning both Jews and Gentiles to faith in Jesus Christ, 1 Peter offers a behavioral strategy that may also be effective. Wives do not submit solely because society demands it, but because it may be evangelistically effective. When evangelizing, actions oftentimes speak louder than words, especially when the evangelist has little social clout. Wives may win over unbelieving husbands without preaching to them. Wives, therefore, are given an important and challenging mission.

Wives who did not worship their husband's gods could be seen as being in rebellion. Therefore, when these wives submit to their husbands it could minimize any backlash that might come their way. Indeed, the command to wives is similar to 1 Peter's admonition in 2:12-17 that everyone—not just slaves and wives—employ upright behavior as a way to witness for Jesus.

The similarity of the argument of 3:1-6 and 2:12-17 is reinforced by 1 Peter's unique vocabulary. It is only in 2:12 and 3:2 that he uses the verb *epopteuō*, a word that occurs nowhere else in the NT. The basic meaning of *epopteuō* is "I pay close attention." The cognate, *epoptēs*, occurs only once in the NT, in 2 Pet 1:16, with the sense of "eyewitness." Throughout 1 Peter, and particularly in the arguments of chapters two and three, the author stresses that the Christian community is under scrutiny by those on the outside. And those on the outside can be hostile. Yet outsiders may be won to the faith, including husbands who scrutinize the pure and respectful behavior of their wives.

Conclusion

The phrase at the start of 1 Pet 2:21, "for to this you have been called" points back to the abuse described in v. 20, and indicates that suffering is not meaningless; it serves a purpose. That purpose is found when considering the suffering of Christ.

Indeed, in 1 Pet 2:21-25 we read how suffering characterized the ministry of the Messiah. What Christ went through on earth was for others—even slaves—and provides an example for encouragement and motivation. First Peter 2:21-25 focuses upon the catalytic impact that suffering can have; i.e., in the same way that Christ serves as an example for Christian slaves because he endured unjust treatment, the attitude of these slaves during the heat of oppression can also be a witness to onlookers (1 Pet 2:15). Slaves are called to follow in the footsteps of Christ as 1 Pet 2:24-25 does not emphasize the resurrection of Christ, but rather his death.

The message to aliens, exiles, slaves, and woman—non-citizens and second-class citizens, is that the way of Christ is the way of suffering. Joel Green points out that "the combination of these words 'Christ' and 'suffering,' a commonplace in 1 Peter, is nonetheless jarring."[174] Green goes on to note: "Whereas the word 'christ' had the basic sense of 'anointed one,' and whereas in the traditions that had developed from the Scriptures of Israel, the term would have signified the most honorable status for God's envoy, for Peter 'christ' is unmistakably enmeshed in conventional notions of dishonor and rejection. Nevertheless, it is precisely this ignominious suffering and death that is effective for liberating God's people. And it is this humiliated, spurned Christ whom God vindicates, raises up, and enthrones."[175]

Non-citizens and second-class citizens know well the pain of suffering. That was so in the world of 1 Peter's readers and arguably has typically been true throughout time. Furthermore, 1 Peter shows us that the way of Christ is characterized by suffering and rejection. Therefore, we may appreciate that the non-citizen and second-class citizen followers of Christ are uniquely qualified to teach us the way of Jesus.

Our own nation's history is replete with stories of immigrants, slaves, and women whose faith not only sustained them through suffering, but also served to be a testimony to others. In my pulpit ministry, I often share the story of my own family members, especially that of my great aunt, a member of the African diaspora who was raised picking cotton in South Carolina. Flossie Glenn eventually moved to Washington, DC, met the man who would become her husband, and was married to Clifton Johnson for 65 years. We overlapped in Washington, DC for many years and Aunt Flossie once responded to one of my questions by saying, "Don't you know all the females in your family did domestic work for white people?" She endured the Jim Crow south and worked most of her life as a maid and cook, caring for other people's children while raising her own children. At her funeral, the eulogist, a 68-year-old retired federal judge who met my great aunt when he was born, regaled us with stories of her great faith and love toward others. My great aunt, a victim of a racist, patriarchal society, a second-class citizen all her life, nevertheless taught many a way of life consistent with the so-called Golden Rule.

Poor or poorly educated people are not merely inspirational; they are educational. They are our teachers. My encouragement, from a missional perspective, is that the Church does well to increase its attention to those on the margins because it is there that we often see Christ most clearly. Perhaps the best teacher for Christians is not the powerful in society, not the model citizen, but those whose association to the State has been questioned and scrutinized the most because of their lowly position in society. These are citizens worthy of the gospel.

BIBLIOGRAPHY

Achtemeier, Paul J. *Peter 1 Hermeneia*: *A Critical and Historical Commentary on the Bible*. Minneapolis, MN: Fortress Press, 1996.

Balch, David. *Let Wives Be Submissive: The Domestic Code in I Peter*. Chico, CA: Society of Biblical Literature, 1981.

Barton, Stephen C. "Social Setting of Early Non-Pauline Christianity." In *Dictionary of the Later New Testament & Its Developments,* edited by Ralph P. Martin and Peter H. Davids. Downers Grove: IVP Academic, 1997), 1108.

Beard, Mary. *SPQR: A History of Ancient Rome*, *1st ed.* New York, NY: Liveright, 2015.

Bechtler, Steven Richard. "Following in His Steps: Suffering, Community, and Christology in 1 Peter." In *Society of Biblical Literature*, 1998.

Campbell, Barth L. *Honor, Shame, and the Rhetoric of 1 Peter*, 1st edition. Atlanta: Scholars Press, 1998.

Cohick, Lynn H. "Philippians and Empire: Paul's Engagement with Imperialism and the Imperial Cult." In *Jesus Is Lord, Caesar Is Not: Evaluating Empire in New Testament Studies*, ed. Scot McKnight and Joseph B. Modica, 166. Downers Grove, IL: IVP Academic, 2013.

Edwards, Dennis R. "Good Citizenship: A Study of Philippians

1:27 and its Implications for Contemporary Urban Ministry." In *Ex Auditu 29*, 2013.

_____. *Might from the Margins: The Gospel's Power to Turn the Tables on Injustice* (Harrisonburg: Herald Press, 2020).

Elliott, John H. "Disgraced Yet Graced: The Gospel According to 1 Peter in the Key of Honor and Shame." In *BTB* 25 (1995): 166-78.

_____. *1 Peter: A New Translation with Introduction and Commentary*, First Edition AB. New York, NY: Anchor Bible, 2001.

Green, Joel B. *1 Peter*. Grand Rapids, MI: Wm. B. Eerdmans Publishing Co.

Jobes, Karen H. *1 Peter*. In Baker Exegetical Commentary on the New Testament, Grand Rapids, MI: Baker Academic, 2005.

Michaels, J. Ramsey. *1 Peter, Volume* 49. (Grand Rapids: Zondervan, 2015), 138.

Thurman, Howard. *Jesus and the Disinherited*. Boston, MA: Beacon Press, 1996.

Volf, Miroslav, "Soft Difference: Theological Reflections on the Relation Between Church and Culture in 1 Peter." In *Ex Auditu* 10, 1994.

4

UNDIVIDED WINGS:
Engaging Patristics Through Gospel Haymanot

VINCE L. BANTU

The fourth-century, Syriac-speaking, poet-theologian Ephrem the Syrian said that "Truth and love are wings undivided. Truth cannot fly without love. Love cannot soar without truth.

Their yoke is one of unity."[176] The Syrian deacon and *malphono* ("teacher") of the Church of Urhoy (Edessa) wrote theological poetry in which he defended biblical orthodoxy in an accessible manner for his cultural context. However, Ephrem understood that Christian orthodoxy was incomplete if it is unaccompanied by a lifestyle of justice and mercy. Despite living much of his life in a monastic cell in the environs of Urhoy, a severe famine in the city drew him into service that resulted in the saving of countless Syrian citizens and cost Ephrem his life.[177] Ephrem was not unique to early Christianity in his understanding of the implications of the Gospel on belief and action. As Peter Brown has noted, "what early Christians took for granted, as part of an inherited conglomerate of notions shared with Judaism, was that they were responsible for the care of the poor of their own community."[178]

This essay will approach the discipline of patristic Christian history from the perspective of a Gospelist historical theologian, emphasizing two central points: 1.) Christian theology has found holistic expression—upholding the interdependent values of theological orthodoxy and social justice—since the earliest centuries of the Church. After the increasing Hellenization of Christianity among Roman imperial authority, it was ancient African and Asian Christian communities that continued to promote holistic ministry and theology. The integrated approach to Christian God-talk—or, Gospel Haymanot—that has defined the faith of Black Christians finds resonance in ancient African and Asian Christian traditions. The binary of contemporary Western Christendom that divides theological truth from social liberation is complicated by the theological imagination of African-descended Christians—both ancient and modern. 2.) The subaltern voices of patristic Christianity complicate common assumptions regarding the early Church's relationship to empire and reveal the foundations of an integrative view of the Gospel that has been echoed among marginal Christian communities in the modern world.

As an African-American scholar of early Christianity, I often find myself traversing the same bifurcated theological climate that has been described throughout this volume: theological communities that emphasize either the universal truth of the Gospel or its implications for liberation for the marginalized. In the context of teaching and researching in patristics, I find myself rooted in a Gospel Haymanot perspective of the lived Black church that complicates conservative attempts of a wholesale embrace of Greco-Roman doctrinal history as well as the liberal claim that orthodoxy is inextricably bound to imperial domination.

I recently experienced both of these extremes in one day: after teaching a course on early Christianity at a conservative, white evangelical seminary, several of the students rejected the idea that the Miaphysite Christian communities of Egypt, Syria, Ethiopia, and Armenia were not real Christians because of their rejection of the Council of Chalcedon (a council these students held to be inspired and led by the Holy Spirit). Later that day I flew to a gathering of predominately Black scholars of religion and theology. After the workshop ended, several of us went out for a drink and ended up in a debate where I was countering the claim (held by almost the entire group) that the practice of evangelism and concepts such as orthodoxy and heresy are products of oppressive groups in the service of domination. Experiences such as these illustrate briefly how a Black patristics scholar committed to biblical orthodoxy and Black liberation will struggle to find a place in the current climate of theological education. It is for this reason that the following study will emphasize the holistic foundation of the Christian faith and the persistence of a counter-imperial Christian identity.

The Christianization of the Roman Empire during the fourth century was vividly depicted in the panegyric *Life of Constantine*. Written by the Caesarean bishop and historian Eusebius, this work of propaganda embellishes the elevation of Christianity as the Roman religion following the alleged conversion of Emperor Constantine (306-337 CE). This biography represents one of the first major efforts in Roman Christianity in understanding the Empire as God's agent in the world:

> Thus, like a faithful and good servant, did he act and testify, openly declaring and confessing himself the obedient minister of the supreme King. And God forthwith rewarded him, by making him ruler and sovereign, and victorious to such a degree that he alone of all rulers pursued a continual course of conquest, unsubdued and invincible, and through his trophies a greater ruler than tradition records ever to have been before. So dear was he to God, and so blessed; so pious and so fortunate in all that he understood, that with the greatest facility he obtained the authority over more nations than any who had preceded him.[179]

While the historical reliability of the *Life of Constantine* remains unclear, Eusebius' theological imagination of the first Christian Emperor of Rome betrays an emergent imperial Christianity that would come to dominate much of Roman Christianity. Indeed, Roman Christianity became increasingly deployed as a mechanism for identifying Roman civil identity—in a manner similar to the function of pre-Christian Roman *religio*.[180] The advent of the Christian state in the fourth century had two implications on Roman Christianity: Roman

Christians now saw themselves as part of the dominant culture and began to expect a society governed by Christian principles. As Roman Christianity formed the foundations of the Western World, the version of Christianity that emerged from this part of the world—which has since been seen as synonymous with Christianity itself—became characterized by two corresponding traits: mainstream Christian theology assumed the perspective of the socially privileged and Christian rulers were understood to represent the will of God on earth. The results of these Roman insertions into biblical theology was the reduction of justice rhetoric to an emphasis on charity and theological justification for state-sponsored oppression.

The fourth-century theologian Gregory of Nazianzus displays a perspective regarding the poor common to Late Antique Christianity in his sermon *On the Love of the Poor*. Gregory was born in the region of Cappadocia to wealthy Christian parents and he later became the bishop of Constantinople and one of the most influential Roman theologians in antiquity. Like many of his contemporaries, Gregory stressed the duty of Christians to care for the poor in a manner that juxtaposes "the poor" with "Christians":

> Give something to God in thanksgiving that you are of those who can give help, not of those who stand and wait for it; that you have no need to look to another's hands, but that others must look to yours. Grow rich, not only in substance, but also in piety; not only in gold, but also in virtue; or rather, only in virtue. Be more honoured than your neighbor, by showing more compassion. Be as God to the unfortunate, by imitating the mercy of God.[181]

Gregory's connection of charity with the attributes of God—and elsewhere with the Incarnation—represents the period when Christian charity began to envision the "giver" in a role analogous to God. Throughout his homily, Gregory consistently contrasts the poor "they" with the Christian "us," giving the impression of a significant distinction between the two groups. In this passage Gregory displays two aspects of an imperial theological perspective regarding poverty and justice: theological reflection comes from a place of dominance and the work of justice is to give charity. Gregory was deeply influenced by the monastic movement which stressed giving to the poor and was, to a significant degree, a reaction to imperial Christianity. Gregory even questioned whether poverty was the result of divine punishment:

> Whether it comes from God that these should be tormented is not yet manifest; just as it is not manifest whether this corruptible body of itself brings forth this irregularity, in its course as it were. And who knows whether this man is being punished because of his wickedness, and this other uplifted as good and worthy of praise, and not the contrary: that this man is being uplifted because of his wickedness, and this other is being tested because of his virtue?[182]

However, the earliest Christians had a clear understanding of the cause of poverty. As the Apostle James rhetorically asks, "Is it not the rich who are exploiting you?" (Jas. 2:6). The New Testament consistently expresses a theological sociology that takes into account the presence of Satan in world governments. Jesus and Paul refer respectively to the devil as the "ruler" (*archon*) and "god" (*theos*) of this world (Jn. 14:30; 2 Cor. 4:4). While the biblical authors make clear the responsibility of governmental authorities to submit to the ultimate rule of God (Rom. 13:1-7), they were under no illusions regarding the reality of demonic influence in state activity. In his apocalyptic visions, John the Evangelist describes the Roman Empire as a dwelling of demons and its economic exchanges with political authorities and venture capitalists with the imagery of adultery (Rev. 18:1-3). John takes the Satanic provenance of Rome's opulence as a given. God's People, however, are called to "come out of her" so that they "will not share in her sins" (Rev. 18:4). Through its powerful imagery, the book of Revelation stands in the great company of early Christian texts, which understood systemic oppression as the cause of poverty. Amidst the copious amounts of studies on wealth and poverty in early Christianity, it is surprising that few have focused on how early Christians viewed the *cause* of poverty.[183] Following the dawn of imperial Christian theology, discourse regarding poverty was largely relegated to charity among dominant Christians. However, the early Church—as expressed in texts written by and for the oppressed—knew that systemic oppression was a reality.

Earliest Christianity emerged from the perspective of those on the periphery of society. For this reason, the earliest voices of the Church took for granted a social position of marginality; divinely-instituted social hegemony was not in the realm of possibility. Rather, the first Christians assumed the presence of spiritual darkness at work among imperial powers and understood the role of God's people on earth to be a witness to His righteousness and justice.

Beginning in and following the fourth century, a counter-narrative in Christian theology began which understood God's people to occupy the positions of social dominance. Imperial Christianity has been a prominent mechanism in the maintenance of dominance—as in the case of the Trans-Atlantic Slave Trade, Jim Crow segregation, and mass incarceration. However, the Gospel has given voice to countless oppressed people in rejection of oppressive, imperial theology. The Church of the modern world is a peculiar one that is made up of some of the most powerful humans who believe God has divinely destined them to rule and some of the most oppressed people in the world who trust in Jesus for their liberation from sin and injustice. The latter, however, more closely resembles earliest Christianity.

It is common among many conservative, Western theologians to understand the earliest ecumenical councils as divinely inspired or, in some way, guided by the hand of God. In his description of the schism following the Council of Chalcedon (451 CE), Bruce Shelley, utilizing the inappropriate label "Monophysite" in reference to the historic faith of many African and Asian Christians, describes the Christological convictions of Miaphysite Christians as a "sad" theological trajectory. Shelley describes the Chalcedonian formula of Christ existing in "two natures" as the only consistent expression of biblical orthodoxy: "The merit of the Chalcedonian statement lies in the boundaries it established. In effect, it erected a fence and said, "Within this lies the mystery of the God-man. Fifteen hundred years after the event we may wish for more understandable terms, but we dare not say less than the church said then."[184] Typical of white evangelical historiography, Shelley's treatment of Miaphsyite doctrine lacks engagement with the African and Asian primary sources.

This is evidenced in the inaccurate summary of Miaphysite Christology: "They (Miaphytsites) held that instead of the divine and human natures joining to form one person in Jesus, he possessed but one nature in which divine life and human were indistinguishable."[185] However, distinction between the persons of Christ has been affirmed by the largest body of Miaphysite Christians in the modern world—the Coptic Orthodox Church of Egypt: "Neither did the Divine nature transmute to the human nature, nor did the human nature transmute to the Divine nature. The Divine nature did not mix with the human nature nor mingle with it, but was a unity that led to Oneness of Nature."[186] The twentieth-century Pope of Egypt Shenouda clarifies the position of the Coptic Church on the nature of Christ which stands in continuity from the Popes who resisted Western Chalcedonian theology from the beginning.

After the Roman Church excommunicated and exiled the Egyptian Pope Dioscorus, his successor Timothy Aelurus composed a treatise refuting the Council of Chalcedon called *Against Chalcedon*. In this text, Timothy wrote to support the Egyptian Church in their belief "in God the Father Almighty and in Christ Jesus his only son our Lord who was born of the Holy Ghost and the Virgin Mary."[187] This Timothy refers to the "unchanging profession which the whole assembly of the faithful makes" and the view that is in line with Scripture. The concern of the earliest Miaphysites who resisted the Western Chalcedonian formula was not political nationalism nor was it to dissolve the distinction of the natures of the incarnate Christ. Rather, the primary texts written in Syriac and Coptic reveal a desire to resist theological innovations that are extra-biblical. It is entirely inaccurate to represent the Miaphysite faith as one that diminishes or dissolves the humanity of Christ. Writing immediately after the Islamic Conquest of Egypt in the mid-seventh century, the Pope of Egypt Benjamin comments on the humanity of Christ in a sermon written in Coptic:

> I believe that my Savior did everything that is normal for a man except sin alone. I believe that he was hungry— he, the satisfaction of those who hunger. I believe that he was thirsty—he, the quenching of everyone who thirsts. I believe that he tolerated everything for the sake of humanity. I believe that he went to the feasts, ate, drank, and celebrated with the guests and that he changed the water into wine—not in appearance, but

in reality. My beloved, let us not trust the heretics, lest they mislead us and take us to perdition with them.[188]

To the contrary of centuries of Western Christian caricatures of early African and Asian theology, Egyptian theologians not only affirmed the full humanity of Christ but even argued its importance against local Egyptian heretics who denied the full humanity of Christ. The majority of Church history textbooks written by and for the Western Christian world misrepresent non- Western theologies (ancient and modern) and often do not engage primary sources written in languages other than Greek and Latin.[189] The fact that Western Christianity consistently condemns theological perspectives that haven't even been read in their own words is a consistent manifestation of white supremacy: that which is foreign and unfamiliar is rejected or denigrated as unsophisticated.[190] I have taught and lectured in countless white Christian contexts where evangelicals who have never heard the names Timothy Aelurus, Jacob of Serugh, or Benjamin of Alexandria—much less read their writings—are nonetheless already committed to the idea that these Christians are heretics because some evangelical Church history textbook told them so. It is also likely that said Church history textbook did not include primary engagement with Miaphysite sources in Coptic, Syriac, Armenian, or Ethiopic.

The words of Benjamin also complicate the theological historiography of white liberal theology—and its subsidiary often known as "Black theology." Benjamin held his fellow Egyptians who minimized the humanity of Christ as heretics. Early Christians across the Roman, Persian, Ethiopian, Chinese, Nubian, and Indian Empires all had a concept of orthodoxy and heresy—this was not a Western Christian innovation.

Following the influential work of Walter Bauer, patristic scholars understand the concept of orthodoxy having not been clearly defined before the fourth century as the Christian world was filled with divergent theologies.[191] Christians and the various Christian-derived religions (Gnosticism/Valentianism, Marcionism, Manichaeism, Montanism, Docetism) were all minorities in the Roman and Persian Empires and therefore, no specific expression of Christianity experienced dominance before the fourth century.

Following the reforms of Constantine establishing Christianity as the dominant religion of the Roman Empire, Christianity as it was expressed in the Greco-Roman world became seen as the quintessential expression of Christianity. Roman Christianity began to take on many aspects of Hellenistic culture. The theological formulas of the councils of Nicaea, Constantinople, Ephesus, and Chalcedon were laced with extra-biblical, Hellenistic terminology (*ousia*/"person"; *prospon*/"face"; *hypostasis*/"essence"; *physis*/"nature"). The appropriation of Greek philosophical terminology to articulate the mysteries of the Gospel were not a new invention. Even the New Testament deploys Hellenistic terms (*logos*/"word/discourse") to describe the nature of God and His activity in the world. However, the fourth century witnessed the beginning of the "Western cultural captivity of the Church"[192] in that Christian orthodoxy was now seen as valid only when articulated by the norms of the Greco-Roman world.

The beginning of this Western Christian identity politic would take greater shape during the times of the Holy Roman Empire, Crusades, and Western Colonialism and constitute the most significant barrier to Christian mission today—the association of Christianity being a white/Western religion and, therefore, unfitting for non-white/Western people. The role that early doctrinal development played in this dynamic can hardly be an act of God's will. Many of the creeds articulated orthodox, biblical theology regarding the Father, Son, Holy Spirit, Scripture, salvation, and the Church all while using Roman terms and concepts befitting the local context.

This is a good thing. The problem is when the Western way of doing theology is promoted as the only legitimate means for all.

The Nicene term *homoousias*—which was used to argue the full equality of the Father and the Son—was largely promoted as the standard of orthodox theology. However, in the Syriac-speaking milieu of Urhoy (Edessa), Ephrem the Syrian chose to reject this foreign term and express the equality of the Father, Son, and Holy Spirit in Syriac terms more fitting for his Syrian context.[193] One century later, Ephrem's Syriac Christian successors were rejected as heretics by the dominant Roman Church for their continued practice of articulating Miaphysite ("one-nature") Christology according to their socio-cultural context. These facts represent three dynamics relevant to a Gospelist reading of patristic sources: the emergent Western Church exercised social dominance that caused Christianity to flourish in the West and decline in Africa and Asia; dominant Western Christianity introduced a perceived division between social justice and theological orthodoxy; there remained a Gospel-centered trajectory of Christian theological discourse embracing doctrinal orthodoxy and social justice concurrently with the counter narrative of imperial theology which was not reflected in the New Testament or earliest Christian witness.

Like the Church of the Book of Acts, earliest Christianity would have found the notion that the Kingdom of God supports the interests of empire as foreign as the idea that the teleological aim of the Gospel is social liberation for the oppressed alone without the necessity of orthodox doctrine. Modern theologians have been significantly influenced by the

Fundamentalist-Modernist controversy—and its later-twentieth century manifestations—and read early Christian history through the lens of the modern, bifurcated vision of Christian witness.[194] On the one hand, the tendency among conservative scholars exists to place a blind stamp of divine approval on early doctrinal formation emanating from the imperial Church. The complicity of the imperial Church throughout the development of the Western World is overlooked or dismissed as a necessary casualty for the spread of the Gospel. On the other hand, liberal scholars—wisely attuned to the problematic nature of dominant Christianity—often make two mistakes: the false assertion that orthodox doctrine was an imposition of the imperial Church and that earliest Christians did not hold exclusive claims about Jesus' person and work.

Ironically, many liberal scholars advance white supremacist narratives of Christian history by only appealing to Western Christian sources. The languages and cultures of Africa, the Middle East, and Asia produced some of the earliest and most profound Christian literature. Yet many liberal, Black scholars do not familiarize themselves with these sources, looking only to the Greek and Latin writers. However, the Christian theology that emerged in African and Asian languages represent a Gospel Haymanot that holds firmly to truth and justice. Even in Greek and Latin sources that emerged from the context of the mainstream imperial Church, a Gospel Haymanot continued to emerge and speak against the dominant Roman Church that was increasingly characterized by aligning itself with positions of social dominance. There is perhaps no better example of the development of Gospel Haymanot in the post-imperial early Church than the development of the Christian monastic movement. Indeed, the wide-scale development of Christian ascetic practices has been commonly understood as a reaction against the advent of imperial Christianity.

The early Church in the Roman Empire was characterized by persecution and martyrdom. Suffering for the cause of Christ was held as an honor and the highest form of worship. After Roman Christians became part of the mainstream culture and life for Roman Christians became more comfortable, ascetics desired to leave lives of comfort and continue to live a life of Christian sacrifice.[195] This is demonstrated uniquely in Egypt as the commemoration of martyrs—or the cult of the saints—became increasingly "monasticized" as martyr shrines began to be intricately connected to ascetic communities in late antique Egypt.[196] As monasticism came into Christianity from Judaism, these communities of ascetics first emerged most prominently in Syria and Egypt. Christian monasticism soon became an integral part of African Christianity in Nubia, North Africa, and Ethiopia. Likewise, Syrian asceticism spread into the Persian Empire and from there, across Central, South, and East Asia. Monasticism also spread across the Roman Empire and even to the furthest regions of Europe. John Cassian served as a bridge between Africa and Europe when he learned the monastic practices of Egypt and introduced them in Western Europe.

Beginning with the communal (or cenobitic) form of monasticism that developed principally through the work of an Egyptian ascetic named Pachomius, monasteries throughout late antique Christianity epitomized a Gospelist approach to Christian thought and activity.

Especially in Egypt, monasteries represented the most significant centers that influenced much of the theology and social life of the Egyptian Church. Monasteries were centers of social justice and community development as they were often filled with converts to Christianity who had converted from pagan Egyptian religion. In Upper Egypt, traditional Egyptian religion was often associated with wealthy landowners while many of the Christians in the monasteries were from lower income backgrounds. The monasteries provided employment, education, and a sense of community for early Egyptian Christians—much like the role played by the African-American church since its inception.

Monastic leaders such as Shenoute of Atripe (347-465 CE) would critique wealthy landowning pagans nearby who oppressed the poor and attempted to use their social position to enforce pagan religion. The most prominent example of this was the protest that Shenoute led against a wealthy Roman governor named Gesios. Like many wealthy politicians in the employ of the Roman Empire, Gesios exploited the labor and resources of the majority population which was primarily low-income. Leading his monastic community of Egyptian Christians, Shenoute protested against Gesios prominently in his public sermons: "For just as you are godless, so you afflict the poor with your abusive acts."[197] Shenoute began his sermon with an invective against Gesios' pagan religious practices. Despite publicly claiming to be a Christian, Gesios secretly worshipped Roman pagan gods, a fact that Shenoute desired to expose.

The two primary issues that Shenoute addressed to the governor Gesios were: the governor's imposition of pagan religious practices on the Egyptian Christians and his exploitation of the poor. These two concerns also happen to be the most oft-mentioned sins in the Bible: idolatry and oppressing the poor. These dual concerns provide the premise for the greatest commandments: to love the Lord with all of one's being and to love one's neighbor as self (Matt. 22:36-40). The inextricable nature of love of God and love of neighbor forms the core of Gospel Haymanot. Early African Christians such as Shenoute understood the call on the People of God to live as a witness to the lordship of Jesus Christ being realized by right worship and right treatment of neighbor. Shenoute advocated on behalf of the Upper Egyptian community of Shmin (Panopolis) and the Christians of his monastic community.

The overwhelming majority of the monks of Shenoute's White Monastery had come from poverty before entering the monastery to be instructed in orthodox theology and receiving employment, housing, health care, and access to food. Like many Roman governors in Egypt, Gesios had been imposing Roman pagan religion among the Christians by requiring them to construct Roman religious bath houses and paying the workers in wine used for pagan ceremonial purposes. Gesios was inhibiting Christian worship by prohibiting the believers from celebrating the Pasch (Easter). Shenoute also lists numerous ways in which the governor had been oppressing the poor including the confiscation of property, excessive imposition of taxes, and unfair wages:

> Are the villages (your) workers' settlements? You didn't build their houses in them, did you? And yet these same afflictions (those of a workers' settlement) are the things with which you torment them, with your forced labors, your foul wines, all your oppressions, and your abusive acts, O you people whom that voice threatens,

"as for the contentious ones who disobey the truth but who obey unrighteousness—wrath, anger, affliction, and oppression be upon every human soul that works for evil!"[198]

The theological perspective of Shenoute and many early Christian ascetics called for the exclusive lordship of Christ to be lived out in society through the presence of social justice. The Gospel was lived out in this context as the monastery was a source of social dignity, economic empowerment, and centers of instruction in theological orthodoxy. After the dominant Roman Church rejected the majority of Christians in Africa, the Middle East, and Asia following the Council of Chalcedon (451 CE), the monastic centers of Egypt, Nubia, Ethiopia, Syria, and Persia served as the most important centers for asserting the independent theological identity of African and Asian Christians. Therefore, it is inaccurate to claim that Western Church councils were divinely inspired defenses of biblical theology. The disagreement that divided the Western Church from the churches of Africa and Asia in the fifth century was over theological language regarding the nature of Jesus' humanity and divinity. Yet, no side in this debate has ever denied the full humanity and divinity of Christ—they were and still are all Christians.

Much of conservative evangelical church history in the Western world often gives cursory attention in the textbooks to these communities or inaccurately misrepresent their theology through the lens of Western misunderstandings of their theology (which was increasingly written in languages Greek and Latin ecclesiastics didn't understand). However, the monastic centers of Africa and Asia were also centers of theological output and biblical orthodoxy. It is equally inaccurate to claim that early

Christians did not hold to exclusive claims about Christ and salvation or that these ideas came from the Roman Empire.[199] From the very beginning, Christians in the Roman and Persian Empires—as well as neighboring empires such as India and Ethiopia—believed in the exclusive truth of the lordship of Jesus Christ. In many cases—such as Egypt, Syria, India, and Persia—the Gospel came in even before Christianity was the dominant religion of the Roman Empire.

In other cases—such as Ethiopia and Arabia—Christianity was introduced during the time of the heretical Arian Roman Emperor Constantius. However, the attempts of Constantius to impose Arian theology (i.e., the belief Jesus was a created being) failed and the monarchs of Arabia and Ethiopia decided to embrace orthodox theology taught by their own indigenous leaders. Christians across the known world argued that Jesus was God and that faith in Him is the only way to salvation. They did this at great personal cost and willingly rejected the pagan religions of their lands. This happened not only long before the Roman Empire became a "Christian Empire," but it occurred at a time when the Romans were persecuting Christians for their exclusive beliefs. In fact, when the Roman Empire was a dangerous place for Christians to live during the second and third centuries, the Persian Empire (modern Iraq, Iran, and Afghanistan) was a much safer place for Christians to thrive.

Therefore, it is inaccurate to claim that Christian doctrine—before the Romanization of Christianity—was unconcerned with matters of theological orthodoxy[200]. Earliest Christians across the known world lived centered on the belief that the Gospel of Jesus Christ is the supreme and only truth—and that this Gospel is not fully realized apart from the empowerment of the most marginalized. Even after this narrative was complicated by the introduction of imperial Christianity, holistic Gospel Haymanot has been an ever-present witness to biblical orthodoxy. The theological genius of Black slaves and Civil Rights leaders was ultimately not an innovation; rather, the Gospel approach of Black Christians seeking liberation in the context of Christocentric worship is the Black manifestation of a centuries-old Christian tradition rooted in the biblical vision of *shalom*.

BIBLIOGRAPHY

Aelurus, Timothy. *Against Chalcedon*, edited by R.Y. Ebied and L.R. Wickham. In *After Chalcedon: Studies in Theology and Church History Offered to Professor Albert van Roey*, edited and translated by C. Laga, J.A. Munitiz, and L. Van Rompay, 115-166. Leuven: Peeters, 1985.

Bauer, Walter. *Orthodoxy and Heresy in Earliest Christianity*. Philadelphia, PA: Fortress Press, 1971.

Brakke, David, and Crislip, Andrew. *Selected Discourses of Shenoute the Great: Community, Theology, and Social Conflict in Late Antique Egypt*. Cambridge: Cambridge University Press, 2015.

Brown, Peter. *Poverty and Leadership in the Later Roman Empire*. Hanover: University Press of New England, 2002.

_____. *The Rise of Western Christendom: Triumph and Diversity, A.D. 200-1000*, 10th ed. Malden, MA: Wiley-Blackwell, 2013.

Ephrem the Syrian. *Madrashe on Faith*, edited by Jeffrey T. Wickes. Washington, D.C.: The Catholic University of America Press, 2015.

Eusebius of Caesarea. *Life of Constantine*, edited by Averil Cameron & Stuart G. Hall. Oxford: Clarendon Press, 1999.

Friesen, Steven J., "Injustice of God's Will? Early Christian Explanations of Poverty." In *Wealth and Poverty in Early Church and Society*, ed. Susan R. Holman, 17-36. Grand Rapids, MI:

Baker Academic, 2008.

Goehring, James E. *Ascetics, Society, and the Desert: Studies in Early Egyptian Monasticism*. Harrisburg, PA: Trinity Press International, 1999.

Gregory of Nazianzus. "On the Love of the Poor and Those Afflicted with Leprosy." In *The Sunday Sermons of the Great Fathers 4: From the Eleventh Sunday after Pentecost to the Twenty-Fourth and Last Sunday after Pentecost*, edited by M.F. Toal, 56. San Francisco, CA: Ignatius Press, 2000.

Hartog, Paul A. *Orthodoxy and Heresy in Early Christian Contexts: Reconsidering the Bauer Thesis*. Eugene, OR: Wipf and Stock, 2015.

Mathews, Jr., Edward G., and Amar, Joseph P. *The Fathers of the Church: St. Ephrem the Syrian: Selected Prose Works*. Washington, D.C.: The Catholic University of America, 1994.

Mikhail, Maged. "On Cana of Galilee: A Sermon by the Coptic Patriarch Benjamin I." *Coptic Church Review* 23.3 (2002): 66-93.

Moberg, David O. *The Great Reversal: Reconciling Evangelism and Social Concern*, 2nd ed. Eugene, OR: Wipf and Stock, 2006.

Rah, Soong-Chan Rah. *The Next Evangelicalism: Freeing the Church from Western Cultural Captivity*. Downers Grove, IL: InterVarsity Press, 2009.

Shelley, Bruce. *Church History in Plain Language*, 3rd ed. Nashville, TN: Thomas Nelson, 2008.

Shenouda III, *The Nature of Christ*. Cairo: Dar El-Tebaa El-Kawmia, 1997.

Tracy, David. "African-American Thought: The Discovery of Fragments." In *Black Faith and Public Talk: Critical Essays on James Cone's Black Theology and Black Power,* edited by Dwight N. Hopkins, 29-38. Waco, TX: Baylor University Press, 2007.

Turman, Eboni Marshall. *Toward a Womanist Ethic of Incarnation: Black Bodies, the Black Church, and the Council of Chalcedon.* New York, NY: Palgrave Macmillan, 2013.

Wickes, Jeffrey T. *St. Ephrem the Syrian: The Hymns on Faith.* Washington, D.C.: The Catholic University of America Press, 2015.

Woodward, E.L. *Christianity and Nationalism in the Later Roman Empire.* London: Longmans, Green, and Co., 916.

5

WORSHIPPING WHILE BLACK:
A Peace Studies Analysis of Black Church Origins and the Implications for Gospel Haymanot

NICHOLAS ROWE

It was a Sunday in November 1787 at St George's Methodist Church in Philadelphia when Richard Allen, his colleague in ministry, Absalom Jones, and fellow African converts arrived for morning worship. At the door, the sexton gave instructions for them to go to the newly constructed upper-level gallery. They arrived at their seats just as the opening prayer had commenced, and so they knelt in prayer. As Allen related:

> We had not been long upon our knees before I heard considerable scuffling and low talking. I raised my head up and saw one of the trustees, H—M--, having hold of the Rev. Absalom Jones, pulling him up off

of his knees, and saying, "You must get up--you must not kneel here." Mr. Jones replied, "wait until prayer is over." Mr. H—M-- said "no, you must get up now, or I will call for aid and I force you away." Mr. Jones said, "wait until prayer is over, and I will get up and trouble you no more." With that he beckoned to one of the other trustees, Mr. L—S-- to come to his assistance. He came, and went to William White to pull him up.[201]

This forced removal was the latest in a long string of indignities that the Black congregants had to endure. By now, the message was clear that they, distinguished by their Blackness, were no longer welcome in this white-led congregation. After the prayer concluded, Allen and his fellow Africans "all went out of the church in a body, and they were no more plagued with us in the church."[202]

This account will be familiar to some as the critical events that led to the founding of the African Methodist Episcopal (AME) Church, "the institutionalization of black religious independence," as influential scholars C. Eric Lincoln and Lawrence H. Mamiya put it.[203] By merely "worshipping while black," Richard Allen, Absalom Jones, and their congregants became the named predecessors of persons of color whose actions of everyday life become a reason for white discomfort. In a sense, one can say that this was the formal origin of the Black church, formed in a context of rejection by white Christians who would not or could not accept parity and equality with their Black African counterparts. Other Black church collectives arose around specific theological emphases, but the AME's origin narrative, documented in the memoirs of its founder, Richard

Allen, gives historians an insight into dynamics of social identity formation and the dualistic split between confession and behavior that plagues much of American Christian expression to this day.

This interdisciplinary account will consider the events surrounding the formation of the AME as a case study of two vulnerabilities that have persisted in American (and indeed, Western) Christian consciousness and in so doing have limited the religious imagination of Christian communities. In the first, processes of social identity formation can serve to legitimize and justify racial exclusion despite scriptural injunctions against doing so. In the second, one notes the tendency toward dualism where one can separate belief from action. These habits, working in tandem, allowed behaviors that treated Black African members as second-class citizens within the local community. However, Allen, Jones, and other Black leaders desired biblical *shalom* for those to whom they ministered. Their response was informed by what we call *Gospel Haymanot*—an integrated understanding of gospel that dealt with the *whole* person, and which served *all* persons.

In the emerging field of Peace Studies, the nature and resolution of conflict are essential objects of study. The field's analytical frameworks are interdisciplinary, allowing space for both secular and transcendent considerations when looking at causes for historical disputes. Long- term conflicts tend to be deeply entrenched because they become identity-based, particularly around ethnicity or ideology. Opposing parties in these types of conflict often view resolution as an all-or-nothing proposition with a deep fear that loss will result in existential destruction or, at the very least, perpetual subjugation and loss of freedom. It is essential therefore to look at the process of social identity formation and why conflicts with other groups tend to become ones with very high stakes. In other words, what is the nature of the entrenched conflict between competing groups that can result in structures of brutal domination and subjection?

The scriptural presupposition of the nature of persons, the *Imago Dei,* is an important place to begin. The Genesis narrative emphasizes that all humanity is made in the image of God or, said another way, all humanity bears God's image. One of the many and multidimensional results of this is that all humankind, bearing His image, is sacred and all humankind is relational since God is sacred and God is relational. This state of things at creation is by His design and no person exists outside this framework. The narrative then goes on to describe the fall of humanity, the act of rebellion of human ancestors against God's command with the result of relational breakdown between humanity and God and, just as importantly, the break in relationships between human beings (demonstrated by Adam blaming Eve for the whole debacle and not taking full responsibility for his actions).[204] Indeed, one can say all detrimental conflict is a direct consequence of this act.

There are profound consequences to this, chiefly the replacement of the *Imago Dei* (the image of God in the other) with the *imago sui* (the search for the image of myself in the other). Humanity's relational brokenness from the Creator means that people no longer regard Him as the reference for identity or being; the alternative (if the rest of the natural order does not work) is ourselves, or just the self. One evaluates humanity according to how much of one's self one sees in others. If one cannot see that, one either dismisses the humanity of the other or one forces the other to conform to one's own image, always in ways that undermine the dignity of the other (and yes, imperialism, racism, and sexism all fall into these categories).

Insights from social psychology demonstrate the supplanting of the *Imago Dei* with *imago sui*. In the 1980s, Henri Tajfel, along with his student John Turner, suggested a theory for how social group identity gets formed and maintained, especially regarding how groups differentiate themselves from each other (that is, evaluating others as "us" or "them"). They noted that the group to which she belongs could define a person's sense of who she is—an observation that affirms the scriptural idea that persons are inherently relational.[205] Group belonging is a primary source of self-esteem and worth. If the group has status, especially compared to other groups, it enhances its self-esteem. Therefore, there is an investment in helping one's group do well at the expense of others (lowering the standing of competing groups). This means that there is a mental process that takes place where one goes from social categorization (sorting things and people into categories and groups depending upon characteristics and context) to social identification (adopting the hallmarks of the group you have determined yourself to be a part of) and to social comparison (compare "our" group with "other" groups).

For a group to maintain its self-esteem, it needs to compare favorably with other groups. This is critical to understanding prejudice because once two groups identify themselves as rivals, they are forced to compete for the members to maintain their self-esteem.[206] While it is not necessary for this mental process to have such an adverse outcome, it meets the description of the fallen condition of human persons according to Tajfel and Turner's Social Identity Theory.

Rather than looking for the image of God (*Imago Dei*) in other persons, seeking commonality based on being fellow creatures made in God's image, people look for the image of themselves or what they perceive themselves to be in other persons—the image of self (*imago sui*). They do this because they are cut off from the Creator and have no other reference point for personhood. When they do not find their image (the reflection of their social identity) in another, said other becomes less than human or not even human at all. The other becomes a thing, an object to be disposed of or exploited as one wishes. This affirms the corrupted spiritual condition related in the Genesis narrative.

A growing interdisciplinary consensus sheds further light on this dynamic. J. Kameron Carter, theologian and scholar of race and religious studies, links the specter of race to theological origins. The possibility for a racialized imagination comes from the separation of Christianity from its Jewish origins as a process of proto-racial exclusion. The result is that Christianity "was remade into the cultural property of the West."[207] This supersession laid the groundwork for the theological justification of European colonialism.[208] Moreover, as Willie Jennings has shown, the process of colonialism, especially in Africa and the Americas, necessarily put indigenous peoples into a framework that was pre-determined by this theologically framed social identity order. Persons outside the European West were marked, defined, and incorporated into a Western system, otherized not only for being non-Christians but also for being non-Europeans. Race became an easily accessible visual marker for making a hierarchy of persons within this Christendom.[209]

All of this reveals the integrated and totalizing social, political group-identity structures that were at play at St. Georges. The mere presence of a growing Black Christian community challenged the presumption of a Christianity that served as an artifact that was the property of white, Western identity. Whose Christianity was it? Christianity as property of the West required at least a minimal, unobtrusive Black presence compliant with a white-dominant racial social order. When Allen, Jones, and the Black community made demands beyond this, the structure was no longer sustainable. The Black community had to leave in order to be fully and holistically Christian and human.

In observation of the events leading up Mother Bethel's formation, there is extensive evidence that racial *imago sui* was demonstrated by the Philadelphia Methodist Church hierarchy in general, and St. George's Church in particular. First, it appears that the initial summons for Allen to work at the church was to provide a 5:00am worship service for its Black congregants, separate from the regular white service later in the morning. Deliberate segregation already existed as a norm within the white-led congregation. Physical segregation sends two explicit messages from one social-identity group to another. It demarcates a clear distinction between the one and the other. It communicates that there is a clear line between "us" and "them" which is unacceptable to cross. The other message implies that one of these groups controls the space.

Such a line is set up only if one group has the power to enforce it and make it clear that the other is in the space by permission and said permission is tenuous at best. The other is not entitled to the space and has no rights to it. By extension, the control of the space also communicates that the controlling group is superior and the other is inferior. This racial social order was the norm in eighteenth-century American society. The tragic reality was that it was uncritically accepted, even endorsed within this church and the denomination to which it belonged. In stark terms, St. George's white members did not view their Black counterparts through the prism of the *Imago Dei* but through the fearful blinders of their *imago sui*.

Despite the segregated conditions, Allen acceded to this request. The opportunity for ministry beyond the walls of the church burdened him. His pastoral instincts observed, in his words, "a large field open in seeking and instructing my African brethren, who had been a long- forgotten people and few of them attended public worship," and he set about reaching out to the unchurched Black population in the city.[210]

Second, the segregated environment revealed a difference in the philosophy of ministry to unchurched Black people in the city. As the numbers grew, Allen's approach to ministry was decidedly holistic. Not only did he respond to the spiritual needs of his converts, he also addressed their felt needs as well, reflecting an integration of spiritual and physical needs consistent with Gospel Haymanot. Allen does not discuss in his memoirs whether St. George's was involved in any acts of poverty relief or what some call social service ministry today. We do know that the Methodist movement was appealing to non-elite whites because of its simplicity and emotional appeal unlike the rational and formal approach of the Anglican church.[211] However, for Africans and African-Americans in the New World, a chasm remained between the cultural presuppositions of their ancestral homeland and Western presuppositions involving the separation of mind, body, and spirit. Whereas Western Christianity was inclined to observe separations, Allen's ministry assumed the holistic vision of Gospel Haymanot.

In April 1787, Allen collaborated with influential Black Anglican minister, Absalom Jones, and others, founding the Free African Society which attended primarily to the critical material needs of the Black community.[212] This effort was beyond the simple remit of preaching to established Black congregants. As it turned out, Allen's holistic approach was split into two halves.

The physical dimension was handled by the Free African Society while St. George's addressed spiritual needs. This compromised his ministry and it was not long before Allen realized that St. George's was not the proper environment for ministry to Black believers. Not once did Allen mention receiving any assistance from St. George's leadership. He bluntly declares that the presence of Africans "was considered as a nuisance," implying that it was a matter with which the Methodist leadership would rather not have concerned themselves.[213] One can speculate here that, once again, the specter of white *imago sui* was at work with this disregard. One must also wonder if an opportunity to better understand the context of the scriptures was lost by the refusal to learn from an African culture that had more in common with the Hebraic integration of mind and soul than the Hellenistic separation of the two. For, in the imagination of the *imago sui*, the dominant group cannot admit that the subordinated group has something to teach them.

This leads to a third dimension: the white leadership was determined to control and manage the growth of Black membership by forcing it into their segregated social structure. With no formal effort by Methodist officials to meet the holistic needs of converts, Allen attempted to hold informal meetings for Black congregants but the resident elder soon halted these efforts.[214] On more than one occasion, Allen appealed to the Methodist officials for permission to build a church for the new converts but was consistently rebuffed, sometimes with "very degrading and insulting language."[215]

Meanwhile, St. George's was rapidly running out of space. Acknowledging the uneasiness of white parishioners in close quarters with their Black counterparts, ushers first ordered Black members to relinquish their seating on the main floor and to stand along the walls. Not long afterward, the leadership solicited funds from both white and Black parishioners for an expansion project, constructing an upper gallery for extra seating. It was in November that the fateful Sunday occurred. The sexton told Allen and his colleagues where they would sit in the gallery. Was this the newest dimension of segregated space? A refusal of the group in control to physically associate with others in the church? Whatever it was, it appears they took their seats before receiving instruction and it led to a fateful and harsh confrontation. This was the last straw, and the Black members left, never to return.

The ambiguity of Allen's text has raised debates among historians. Was the departure of Black congregants a long-planned action to reveal the racist conduct of St. George's officials, heralding the need for an independent Black church? Or was it an inevitable response to outrageous racist conduct in the middle of worship, from which an independent Black congregation necessarily emerged? Whether Black members were thrown out of the white church or chose to leave, their departure reflects the inhospitable environment that was embodied by this local Christian community.[216]

The dramatic departure was hardly the end of the matter. Allen documents that until the AME Church became an official organization in 1816, repeated efforts were made by elders of the Methodist Church to keep control of the new Black congregation. Allen had come to faith under the Methodists and remained a licensed evangelist of the denomination. He continued to be extremely loyal to their philosophy of ministry if not to their polity. His colleague and lifelong friend, Absalom Jones, was an Anglican. However, both were committed to meeting the holistic needs of Black Philadelphians. Together, they transformed the

Free African Society into the church that would accomplish that goal, Bethel African Methodist Episcopal Church.

One can speculate about the reasons for the recalcitrant behavior of the Methodist hierarchy. With the walkout of a substantial number of congregants, there would be fewer resources from tithes and offerings. However, the Black converts were in no way the wealthiest members of society; indeed, the very existence of a mutual aid society insured limited revenue for the church. If this were merely a matter of saving face it would not account for the demeaning treatment of Black members. A possible explanation is that the process of social identity formation, especially in a competitive context, requires the dominant group to reinforce their place in the social order, filtering entitlement to human dignity through their *imago sui*. In the context of the Methodists and Allen's congregants, Black autonomy was a threat to the white-controlled social order. For Black members to reject white-established norms of space (segregation) and to establish their own space apart from white control was an explicit rejection of the social order.

Furthermore, to have a majority Black congregation within the Methodist denomination implied a measure of parity between its Black and white members, which the latter could not countenance. This would explain the behavior of denominational leadership. Earlier there was the barely disguised contempt at the idea of a church for Black members.[217] Then came the threats of excommunication and manipulation to undermine fundraising for the new building.[218] When that did not work, the local elder refused the request from this Black congregation to send what could only be a white preacher (since only licensed preachers could take the pulpit). This request alone indicated the willingness of Allen and his colleagues to remain within the denomination under some measure of white authority. The elder's refusal, however, was a signal of the white majority's displeasure at the proceedings. Approving Allen's request would not have allowed them to make a play for restoring the social order.

The white Methodists' final attempt was the employment of contractual and legal subterfuge to take over the church property. By this time, the new congregation had lost patience with its denominational leadership. It is telling that, by this point in his narrative, Allen no longer designated them as fellow Methodists but referred to them only as the "white connexion." After initially refusing to appoint a preacher for the church they claimed was part of the denomination, they changed tack and sent an official nominee, only for the Black congregation to dismiss him. The matter finally ended up in court, which ruled in the Black congregants' favor. Allen and the Black congregation were fellow Christians with their white counterparts, sharing the same confession and philosophy of ministry, but under the law, they were no longer beholden to the Methodist Church as an institution.

In his narrative, Allen goes out of his way to identify certain white men who did not get caught up in the vortex of the *imago sui* of white social identity. The life of British-born Francis Asbury, one of the founders of the Methodist Church in North America, intersected with Allen's on some auspicious occasions. Shortly after Allen obtained his freedom, Asbury, along with other leaders in the movement, noted his preaching gifts and appointed him to the circuit. They were the ones who sent him to Pennsylvania, which led to his appointment at St. George's, which, coincidentally, was Asbury's first North American preaching assignment.[219] Following the lead of his mentor, John Wesley, Asbury was quite deliberate about outreach, not only toward white Americans but the African population as well. As a prominent part of the Second Great Awakening, the Methodist philosophy of ministry was particularly well-suited to the latter population. The appeal of Methodism, with its emphasis on experiential salvation, freedom of expression, and especially its emphasis on water baptism, was familiar to the folkways and spiritual experiences of Africans brought to the New World. It also served as an equalizer because rich and free had no greater access to heaven than the poor and enslaved. In this way, converts, having accepted God's gift of eternal life, belonged to a community that corrected for shortcomings and uncertainties of an unjust society. Methodism, as expressed during the revivals and camp meetings, could be used by both free and enslaved Africans to make sense of the world and help create a more humane way of life.[220]

Asbury's deep opposition to slavery arose from his witness of the institution in southern states as well as the influence of his mentor, John Wesley. In his diary, he makes clear his willingness to challenge the institution, citing Wesley's abhorrence of the practice and its contradiction of the principles of the American Revolution. In consequence, Asbury made his thoughts clear: "we therefore think it our most bounden duty to take immediately some effective method to extirpate this abomination from among us."[221] He went so far as to propose that slave ownership ought to disqualify one from church membership. However, the imperative of the American racial order prevailed. Church leaders rationalized that slaveowners would restrict access to enslaved Africans and that the threat of slave rebellion was too much of a social cost. In the words of Pinn and Pinn: "The notion of common redemption or spiritual freedom for all did not mean freedom on earth. Methodist preachers reconciled their concern for enslaved Africans with the demands of slaveholders by emphasizing the saving of the soul irrespective of the physical body's fate."[222]

In addition to making public remarks about his convictions, Asbury demonstrated his commitment to racial equality with his actions. Asbury was not just an institutional patron of Allen; it appears they were also good friends. Richard Newman points out that, on one occasion, Allen went through a sizable expense to purchase a horse to replace Asbury's ailing predecessor.[223] Furthermore, the barrier of race notwithstanding, they shared a lot in common. Both were born into situations of deprivation that produced a temperament that did not take things for granted. They were also both men who took their commitments very seriously: a seriousness about their commitment to God; a seriousness about their conviction that the Gospel was able to save and transform persons; and a seriousness about Scripture that informed how they thought people should engage with each other, especially with regard to race and class.

All this being said, Asbury could be quite ignorant about the dynamics of the racial and social order. An important point in Allen's narrative details the occasion when Asbury invited him along on a preaching circuit to "the slave countries, Carolina and other places."[224] Asbury stipulated that as a free Black man, Allen would not be permitted to associate with the slaves and would have to sleep in a carriage (rather than enjoy proper room and board). Asbury stipulated these conditions not to offend white hosts in a context where a free Black man, by definition, was a threat to the social order. Asbury assured him that, despite these indignities, Allen would have his expenses covered at least. Moreover, Asbury implied that the indignity was a price one paid for the furtherance of the Gospel. Allen demurred. When

Asbury asked why, he conjectured what would take place if either of them fell ill. Despite Asbury's claim of being a simple preacher, and that all he had were "his victuals and clothes,"[225] being a white man of position meant that as a member of the dominant social group with an important social role, he would never be in need.

Through the lens of *imago sui,* the dominant white social group would consider him as one of their own. "Let him be taken sick where he would, he would be taken care of," Allen incisively noted, "but I doubted whether it would be the case with myself."[226] A free Black man, venturing into the slave South, automatically put his most valued possession, his freedom, at considerable risk. Despite Asbury's professional respect and personal friendship, just how much social capital was he willing to expend for Allen? This subtle exchange communicated that a Black man, who through great effort had obtained his freedom, did not think a highly unusual interracial friendship was enough to safeguard it.

Nonetheless, we do know that Asbury's convictions were enough to stand up for his friend, against his tribe, on two critical occasions. In 1794, Asbury, by then a bishop and the leader of American Methodists, dedicated and gave the inaugural sermon at the new African house of worship that would be christened "Bethel."[227] Finally, as if to drive home the point (but certainly not only for that reason), he ordained Allen as the first Black preacher in the Methodist church in 1799.[228] It is very hard not to see these public actions as an implicit rebuke of St. George's Church and the Philadelphia Methodist leadership.

Richard Allen left a legacy of a person who lived out an implicit understanding of Gospel Haymanot, whose "knowledge [was] turned to holy practice," to use the Victorian prose of Charles

Spurgeon.²²⁹ In other words, he did not separate his orthodoxy from his orthopraxis. The struggle of American Christianity has been and continues to be that the powerful impetus of the *imago sui* has corrupted the church, such that the primacy of white identity trumped the scriptural assertion of the unity and inherent equality of all believers. However, we refuse to leave this discussion on this dismal note. Gospel Haymanot is invested with hope. If the inclination of the sinful nature is for people to seek their identity in human-derived cultural choices, then we also know that Scripture will speak the truth about what our true identities are as persons created in the *Imago Dei,* and how that counters all alternatives. Gospel Haymanot must have an explicit confession asserting that our identity as a human race rests on being created in the image of our Creator and being redeemed from our rebellion against Him by our Savior. Furthermore, since identity-based conflict is a global issue, one can proclaim this word anywhere.

The process of social identity formation necessarily creates an ontological wall around a group to define it against all others. In competitive situations where it feels threatened, it also seeks superiority and control over others in the same space.²³⁰ Race and ethnicity, in particular, are potent criteria determining who belongs within a group, and dominant groups have used their race and ethnicity to determine who is fully human and who is not. The narrative that defines the group becomes the norm for all in the contested space. This is the natural tendency in a fallen world. However, when this attempt to define personhood on these terms occurs within the church, it is an affront to the Gospel, because God through Christ has disqualified human customs as the basis for becoming a member of His people.²³¹ The Gospel is the narrative of the church and in that story, God, who created persons and saves persons, defines what it means to be a person.

Scholars in peace and conflict resolution studies, as well as post-conflict practitioners on the ground, stress that a shared story between former combatants is essential for sustained peace after conflict. There must be a shared understanding of the past, including confession and forgiveness, to envision a collective future.[232] This principle rings true with the Gospel. It declares that those "who once were far away have been brought near" both to God, the Creator and Redeemer, and fellow persons with whom we are in existential conflict.[233]

One of the ways the shared Gospel narrative of the future gets articulated is on the human body. Every human body bears the narrative of the *imago sui* that informs the racial social order. One reads the color of a person's skin and this foretells her destiny. However, the counternarrative of the *Imago Dei* was also written on a body; it was written on the body of the God who became a man. With the allegory of Paul in his first letter to the Corinthians, the narrative is written all over the inside of the body which now represents Christ on earth. This allegory outlines the fundamentals of how to form a joint narrative of *shalom* for parties within the church who seek resolution after deep conflict. Discussing this can be quite extensive but the purpose here is to demonstrate how this vision refutes the priorities of the *imago sui* when engaging the other.

First, the *imago sui* establishes the lens through which a community assesses all other groups. To the extent that one is "not like us," they are viewed with suspicion at the very least and with questionable humanity at the very worst. However, within this allegorical body, Paul refutes this presupposition. No one part dominates the others. Just as crucially, the criteria for admission, if one can call it that, is baptism into the Holy Spirit.[234] The implication here is that Jesus is the one in charge; it is His body, and it belongs to no one part of it. The filter, the lens, the perspective, the orientation point is not any member of the created order, but the Creator Himself, and all of the parts submit to Him. There is an implicit affirmation of the *Imago Dei* in Paul's illustration.

Second, the *imago sui* presumes the total independence of the dominant order from the others. The other only has value according to what is assigned to them by the prevailing order. If it decides that the other has used up its worth, the latter can be discarded and replaced. It is the dependence of Empire—subjugated agents are far more dependent upon the metropole than the other way around. However, with the body metaphor, interdependence is non-negotiable:

> The eye cannot say to the hand, "I don't need you!" And the head cannot say to the feet, "I don't need you!" On the contrary, those parts of the body that seem to be weaker are indispensable, and the parts that we think are less honorable we treat with special honor. And the parts that are unpresentable are treated with special modesty, while our presentable parts need no special treatment. But God has put the body together, giving greater honor to the parts that lacked it, so that there should be no division in the body, but that its parts should have equal concern for each other. If one part suffers, every part suffers with it; if one part is honored, every part rejoices with it.[235]

Not only does Paul emphasize the dimension of mutual need, he also affirms the principle of equity, that is, some parts will require different treatment because of something inherent in the part itself. Implicit in this is the idea that justice, an integral part of the *Imago Dei*, is not achieved by forced uniformity or conformity of its members in the image of a dominant element.

As Eugene Peterson puts it in his translation of this passage, "An enormous eye or a gigantic hand wouldn't be a body, but a monster. What we have is one body with many parts, each its proper size and in its proper place. No part is important on its own."[236]

Third, following on from the above, the parts of the body are not generic. This confronts the corollary assumption about the *imago sui*: the inclusion into a context controlled by a dominant order requires all others to conform to the standards and assignments that it sets.

Indeed, Paul makes it clear that the role of each part is not self-determined or determined by other members but is set explicitly by the One who created it: "...God has placed the parts in the body, every one of them, just as he wanted them to be" and "God has put the body together, giving greater honor to the parts that lacked it."[237] Taken another way, and borrowing from another Pauline metaphor, Christ is the head that runs the body.[238] All other parts operate only with reference to the head. If the body represents the Church, the expression of the Kingdom of God, then Christ Himself determines the dominant order, not any of the kingdom's subjects. All other arrangements operate under the *imago sui* and are thus out of order.

Fourth, the body is meant to flourish according to the design and by the will of the One who created it. For this to happen, all its constituent parts must also thrive. Indeed, the welfare of their fellow parts must be a chief concern. God gives particular consideration for more vulnerable parts, "those lacking honor," to make sure there is no discrimination between more esteemed and less esteemed members. Such investment leads to attention and care for vulnerable parts, especially those that are suffering. For "if one part hurts, every other part is involved in the hurt, and in the healing. If one part flourishes, every other part enters into the exuberance."[239]

One of the most insidious parts of the *imago sui* is its process of dehumanization and objectification. The *imago sui* of Europeans created a racial order based on skin color. It questioned the humanity of persons of the African diaspora as well as indigenous persons globally. It justified the objectification of Africans as chattel to serve the purposes of an imposed economy under their control. In this sense, this order severely constrained any possibility of flourishing for Africans and their descendants. As persons bearing the *Imago Dei,* Africans were invested with gifts and abilities to create order and meaning within their local context, with the potentialities for following God's mandate over the rest of creation (even in a fallen state).

However, in the dominant order of European colonialism, these opportunities would rarely find expression as Africans were considered people without civilization and history. Indeed, the assumption of a limited Black intellectual, creative, and authoritative capacity determined (and still determines) the order of the day. Sadly, while some white Christian individuals challenged this presumption, the racialized social and institutional order assumed it to be healthy. It read the wrong narrative about the new order that God is putting together.

The genius and courage of Richard Allen, along with many other Black church founders, is how he recognized the forces of *imago sui* at work within white-dominated American Christian institutions. He quickly saw how it worked for the Philadelphia

Methodists and how it prevented the spiritual and material needs of African believers from being met. As he often stressed, "I saw the necessity of erecting a place of worship for the coloured people,"[240] not in rebellion against the denomination that he forever revered, but against the ways that it was compromised by how their confession did not lead to right action.

A cynic might raise the question as to whether Allen had merely created an inverse racially dominated Christian institution with the space now controlled by Blacks as opposed to whites. Had he and his friends simply conformed to another expression of the *imago sui?* First, while not perfect, one can say that there are very few white persons in Black churches not because of their exclusion, but because of their avoidance. Can white social identity permit submission under the leadership of a person of African descent or organization where said persons predominate? Second, the evidence of Allen's narrative indicated no hostility to white persons and even strong affirmation to those who appeared supportive of his efforts. However, it is essential to remember that the AME Church emerged out of the need to serve African believers well. This did not necessarily mean that white believers could not also be able to receive help and ministry; the doors were open to them as well. Moreover, in his modest style, as a Gospel Haymanot theologian, Allen hints that this was the case. On the occasion of the dedication of the house of worship so longed for, he relates his vision:

> The house was called bethel agreeable to the prayer that was made. Mr. Dickins prayed that it might be a bethel to the gathering in of thousands of souls. My dear Lord was with us, so that there was many hearty Amen's echoed through the house. This house

of worship has been favored with the awakening of many souls, and I trust they are in the *kingdom both white and colored*.[241]

The reference to a multiracial dynamic indicates his commitment to a Christian community beyond the racial constraints imposed by the St. George's context. Perhaps he was able to see the only possible way forward that would safeguard the integrity of Christian orthopraxis: the realization of interdependence as a necessity in Christian communities. May God's people continue to follow this holistic vision.

BIBLIOGRAPHY

Allen, Richard. *The Life, Experience, and Gospel Labours of the Rt. Rev. Richard Allen.* Philadelphia, PA: F. Ford and M.A. Riply, 1880.

Auerbach, Yehudith. "The Reconciliation Pyramid—A Narrative-Based Framework for Analyzing Identity Conflicts." *Political Psychology*, 30.2 (April 2009): 291-318.

Carter, J. Kameron. *Race: A Theological Account.* Oxford: Oxford University Press, 2008.

George, Carol. *Segregated Sabbaths: Richard Allen and the Rise of Independent Black Churches, 1760-1840.* New York, NY: Oxford University Press, 1973.

Jennings, Willie James. *The Christian Imagination: Theology and the Origins of Race.* New Haven, CT: Yale University Press, 2010.

Kelman, Herbert C. "Conflict Resolution and Reconciliation: A Social-Psychological Perspective on Ending Violent Conflict Between Identity Groups." In *Landscapes of Violence: An Interdisciplinary Journal Devoted to the Study of Violence, Conflict and Trauma* 1.5 (2010): 1-9.

Lincoln, C. Eric and Lawrence H. Mamiya. *The Black Church in the African American Experience.* Durham, NC: Duke University Press, 1990.

Long, John Dixon. *Pictures of Slavery in Church and State.* New York, NY: Negro Universities Press, 1969.

Lyerly, Cynthia Lynn. *Methodism and the Southern Mind, 1770-1810*. New York, NY: Oxford University Press, 1998.

Marable, Manning and Leith Mullings. *Let Nobody Turn Us Around: Voices of Resistance, Reform, and Renewal: An African American Anthology*, 2nd ed. Lanham, MD: Rowman & Littlefield, 2000.

Newman, Richard S. *Freedom's Prophet: Bishop Richard Allen, the AME Church and the Black Founding Fathers*. New York, NY: NYU Press, 2008.

Pinn, Anne H. and Anthony B. Pinn. *Fortress Introduction to Black Church History*. Minneapolis: Augsburg Fortress, 2002.

Spurgeon, Charles. *The Power in Praising God*. New Kensington, PA: Whitaker House, 1998.

Tajfel, Henri and John C. Turner. "The Social Identity Theory of Intergroup Behavior." In *Psychology of Intergroup Relations*, eds. S. Worchel, W. G. Austin, 7-24. Chicago, IL: Nelson-Hall Publishers, 1986.

Wang, Zheng. "Old Wounds, New Narratives: Joint History Textbook Writing and Peacebuilding in East Asia." *History and Memory*, 21.1 (2009): 101-126.

Wesley, Charles. *Richard Allen: Apostle of Freedom*. Washington, DC: Associated Publishers, 1935.

6

HOME COOKING:
Evangelical Theology That Includes Us

VINCENT BACOTE

One of the first things I do when teaching theology is to address what I would call "the reputation problem" for words like *theology* and *doctrine*. These are words that some find either intimidating, sleep-inducing, or both. For many, these words strangely connote matters of faith that have little to do with the most important aspects of following Jesus and a lot to do with the minutiae of interest to small tribes of scholars. Part of my strategy in addressing this reputation problem is implementing what I call a "public relations program" for theology. The program begins by admitting there are books and articles one could read that would validate the concerns, followed by re-framing and presenting an alternative understanding of theology and doctrine (e.g., assisting students in understanding it is impossible to truly follow Jesus and not participate in the practice of theology and the formation of doctrine). In my experience as a professor, I have found this to be a highly successful approach.

Yet, there is another reputation problem that needs to be addressed through this public relations program. It is the kind of problem that presents us with the occasion for this event. To frame it as a question: what do you do when theology or doctrine purports to offer good news but yields either insufficient or negative effects? To be more specific, how do we contend with evangelical theology that creates not a crisis that leads to saving faith but experiences of spiritual suffocation or toxicity? Can the reputation of evangelical theology be reframed by a constructive public relations strategy, or is it essentially unable to produce theology and practice that is good news for all? Can evangelical theology be rescued from a reputation that suggests that its proper audience and domain is "for Whites only"?

How does Gospel Haymanot not only shed light on ways evangelicalism is enculturated in white supremacy but also open the way toward an expression of faith that more readily connects theology and ethics (a refusal to keep separate commitments to personal transformation and varieties of biblical social justice)? If "evangel" is in its name, then we (or at least some of us) ought to consider how to refine or rebuild the reputation of evangelical theology so that it leads to a proclamation and practice of Christian faith that is good news for all the nations in general and a theological home for minorities in particular.

Facing the Truth: Revisiting a Crisis

How do we begin to move forward? It will be an exercise in futility if there is not an acknowledgment of the disappointment and frustration numerous minorities have experienced while engaging evangelical theology. While this disappointment is often expressed in the form of personal experiences within evangelical communities, the deficient attention to the theological concerns of non- majority communities is one of the prominent factors involved. Additionally, in some cases, there is either a theological justification given for setting aside these concerns (e.g., the questions either aren't real theological questions or they are expressions of the "social gospel") or the discovery of shocking or lamentable actions, practices, or statements made by prominent figures. To move forward, this reality must be faced and lamented. I will use an episode from my own experience as an example of this experience as well as present a proposal for how we can move forward.

In seminary, as a Christian interested in the connection between theology and public engagement, I was very excited to do an independent study on Abraham Kuyper because I had learned about his contribution to this topic.[242] When I read his 1898 Stone Lectures given at Princeton Seminary, it was not long before I encountered his theology of common grace. When I read about the relationship between common grace and public life, I was very excited that someone gave theological reasons for Christians to be actively involved in theology and the various dimensions of life outside of the church walls. Two pages later, however, I received my first warning sign that complications may lie ahead when Kuyper stated that Africa offered little to the trajectory of human development.243 Three pages later there was even more troubling language:

> From the high-lands of Asia our human race came down in groups, and these in turn have been divided into races and nations; and in entire conformity to the prophetic blessing of Noah the children of Shem and of

Japheth have been the sole bearers of the development of the race. No impulse for any higher life has ever gone forth from the third group.[244]

In this section where Kuyper is making a case for interethnic relations (his language is "commingling of blood") as vital to the development of civilization, he draws on the Curse of Ham language and claims that no contributions to civilization come from Hamitic peoples (certainly this includes Africa). At this point, it may be a surprise to learn that I gave Kuyper the benefit of the doubt; I reasoned that this nonsensical point of view was simply characteristic of many nineteenth-century Christians, and frankly put, silly. I proceeded on to read the rest and was consequently becoming convinced to focus my doctoral dissertation on Kuyper and his theology of public life. However, upon completing the reading of the book, about 6 pages from the end, Kuyper was contrasting election and evolution when he stated:

> To put it concretely, if you were a plant you would rather be a rose than mushroom; if insect, butterfly rather than spider; if bird, eagle rather than owl; if a higher vertebrate, lion rather than hyena; and again, being man, richer than poor, talented rather than dull-minded, of the Aryan race rather than Hottentot or Kaffir.[245]

Now there was no escape. I sat at the desk in a state of disbelief. It doesn't matter the kind of argument Kuyper was attempting to present because there was a clear value judgment made that severely disparaged Africans (I later learned that he made similar statements elsewhere). A crisis was now at hand. What was I to do now? I was so excited about Kuyper's case for a faith that engaged public life. But now, there were no more excuses that could be made for his incredibly problematic language on race. Engagement was now necessary.

Before I share how I addressed this crisis, this is a good place to assert that what I experienced with Kuyper is one version of what many minorities experience within evangelical communities and evangelical theology. There is a "honeymoon phase," a period full of excitement about encountering a community and theology with a strong, central emphasis on the Bible. All is well in this phase, as one learns a lot about the Bible and appreciates being among others who express a firm commitment to faith and Scripture. However, this does not last. For some, the crisis gradually arises out of the learning process as the result of experiencing theological- ethical[246] microaggressions while reading theological works and engaging professors and peers. They at first only raise an antenna but eventually throw the minority student into a quandary of faith and race. For others, a single traumatic event related to faith and race may set off the alarm. For certain, there is a range of experiences that lead to the moment of crisis, but in each case, the moment emerges when evangelical theology seems to be weighed in the balance and found wanting. It is important here to note that these aren't mere intellectual exercises but deeply exasperating experiences, and thoughts of either a divorce or an exodus may occur (e.g., the events associated with the hashtags #ToxicFuller and #BlackExodus–the concerns raised during those events are not unique to Fuller Theological Seminary but have appeared at countless other theological institutions, even mainline ones like Duke Divinity School).

Returning to sharing the handling of my particular crisis, upon facing Kuyper's comments on race, I was now faced with a conundrum: I appreciated having read what was a gateway to Christian engagement in society but was now unsure if I could continue in my doctoral research journey having this racist Dutchman as my dissertation figure. Many thoughts raced back and forth in my mind, including the imaginary scenario of being asked about my devoting time and effort to a theology written by someone who might not have imagined that someone like myself could be capable of study at the highest level. I wondered if it would be a betrayal to continue with Kuyper. Perhaps the obvious and most important question was, "is Kuyper's theology not merely tainted by his statements on race but essentially deficient?" Put differently, is his theology damaged goods and therefore incapable of benefit to someone like myself? Is it true that even the parts of his theology that I liked were intimately connected to racist views?[247] These are difficult, uncomfortable questions that must be addressed if one is to move forward with integrity.

What decision did I make? I considered these questions and concluded to move forward with my dissertation on Kuyper in spite of his views on race. In my judgment, his theological claims related to public engagement were distinct from his troubling commentary on racial superiority.[248] Kuyper was my dissertation figure and has been very helpful for me, but I know he and his theology can only be most beneficial when I am aware of and truthful about his deficiencies. I could only move forward with his theology if I bring forward the good, set aside the bad, recognize the lacunae and do the work of refinement, revision, and renewal to help make it better and more faithful to God than before (note: all of this is to be done with humility, as it is difficult to be completely aware of one's blind spots that may be recognized by others in future generations).[249]

I believe minorities in theology can engage their frustrations with evangelical theology's deficiencies similarly to how I engaged mine with Kuyper's work. To do this with integrity, we must begin by avoiding two extremes in our response. First, we should resist the "denial temptation." Here, with Kuyper, one could argue he should not be judged by contemporary people who fail to recognize he was a man of his time and place. Therefore, his statements were in truth only descriptive examples he employed to make other points. This cannot work because even if true, the contextual clarification will do little if anything to address the shock and distress of persons of African descent who encounter his views on race.[250] While there may be a "legitimate" explanation for these views, it will be difficult to gain a hearing for Kuyper's other sayings if it seems his problematic ones are being defended or characterized as inoffensive. What we cannot deny is the loss of appetite for Kuyper that can occur from reading these words. In the case of evangelical theology, it will do more harm than good to deny the confusion, disappointment, frustration, and (for some) anger that ensues in the face of a theology that is presented as biblical but leaves minority concerns unaddressed or resisted. We can acknowledge contextual limitations to be sure, but not in ways that evade valid criticism of evangelical theology.

Second, we should resist "the dismissal temptation." Using again my engagement with Kuyper as the example, one could immediately (or perhaps eventually) conclude the aforementioned Kuyper quotes indicate Kuyper was not only a racist but also that all of his other contributions are linked to racist commitments and cannot be helpful in any way to non-whites. The obvious problem with this is the refusal to investigate whether these unsettling quotes reveal a particularly sinister ideology present throughout all of Kuyper's work. A rush to summary judgment does not help us to discover the truth. In the case of evangelical theology, we must resist the urge to jettison it as a whole, whether due to the absence of or resistance to theological questions from minorities, or due to problematic views held or practices condoned by evangelical theologians on matters such as race (or related matters like chattel slavery in the modern world).[251] For certain, many have had such negative experiences in evangelical settings that the only reasonable conclusion seems to be an exodus, often to theological institutions and communities where significant attention has been given to their burning questions. I am convinced, however, there are choices beyond the perceived binary of remaining with a frustrating evangelical theology or migrating to more liberal theological shores.

If neither the temptations of denial nor dismissal are adequate, then what is to be the way forward? First, we must be truly critical thinkers. To that end, I propose to begin by taking a cue from those filmmakers such as Steve McQueen, who are known for scenes with long takes. A long take is an uninterrupted shot that may last for several minutes. The camera may move closer or further away, but the camera remains fixed on a place. In *12 Years a Slave*, McQueen said he opted for long takes in the hanging and whipping scenes because it was important that the audience not be "let off the hook," not giving them a chance to look away from the atrocity being committed.[252] In the same way, we must do "long takes" on matters like Kuyper's impertinent words on race, the complexities of race as it has factored into the context of modern theology, as well as the glaring absence of theological content that attends to the minority. We must take great care to see what is there (and not there) and resist the impulses to avert our gaze or seek means of placing a veil over the ugly parts of the past.

When we do this, we need to experience these moments of crisis as not merely an act of disappointment but a practice of lament. We must bring our frustration and distress to God, particularly in instances where members of the Body of Christ have failed us, and perhaps especially when those fellow Christians have seemingly desired to be faithful in their efforts but have been primary or secondary agents of theological malpractice. We should not hold this distress tightly to ourselves, but bring it to God as part of a brazenly honest practice of prayer. This practice of lament is as vital to the practice of theology as intellectual work. After all, the root word for theology (Gr. *Theos*) is "God," and our work is not merely an academic exercise.[253] It is as real as life gets with the God who made us.

As we do these "long takes," to move forward past denial or dismissal, we must be committed to the truth about those who have written evangelical theology, just as I was with Kuyper,[254] recognizing their complexity like the rest of us humans.[255] As we pursue a critical thinking disposition,[256] it is important for Christians to practice obedience to the two greatest commandments.[257] First, by loving God above all other things we must refuse to put any figure on a pedestal and resist projecting Messianic status on them, thus admitting they have or had feet of clay like all of us. Secondly, we are to love our neighbors as ourselves, including those who have been here before us, being willing to treat them as we would have others treat us.

This means having a willingness to look at Kuyper and others truthfully, not only as persons who made mistakes of commission and omission theologically, but also as those who may have important contributions for us, and in cases like

Kuyper, contributions that may undermine the views expressed in the quotes we read at the beginning. Beyond contributions that may be already present in Kuyper or other expressions of evangelical theology, it may also be the case that a tradition has latent or unacknowledged potential for addressing the theological concerns of minorities. Certainly, if evangelical theology purports to be an expression of fidelity to the entire Word of God, at least in theory, it should have something to say to us. As we obey the two greatest commandments, we are on the way to being critical thinkers who put no figure or tradition in the place of God and who strive toward criticism tempered by love for our neighbors even amid their theological deficiencies.[258]

Choosing to Stay… and Have a Say

If we are going to move forward, how might we proceed? To begin, we aim toward a constructive response. We emerge from our lament, resisting the temptations of denial and dismissal with the brutally honest recognition of our disappointment and distress, having reckoned with the shortcomings of theological figures and positions. This descriptive task is important, and it may be the case that some invest most of their time interrogating and describing the faults and deficiencies in evangelical theology (for some this is an exercise in apologetics that helps those in the majority culture to see what is unrecognized or unacknowledged). For others, our aim should not be an exhaustive excavation of all the ways Kuyper and other figures displayed views about racial superiority or resistance to minority concerns; instead, I suggest we do two things:

1. Consider how the work of "typical" evangelical figures might actually provide helpful theological contributions

that encourage the development of a faith that addresses the concerns of minorities, such as an antidote to racism and other forms of social oppression.

2. Venture forward to develop "fill in the gaps" in theology, sometimes by retrieval of the great tradition, other times by presenting theological ideas/developing angles that have been waiting to be articulated in an evangelical key. This constructive task of theology is not a new idea; it is what Christians have done for centuries as the faith has encountered contextual circumstances that called for theological innovations.

In the example of theological reflection from the Black church, which we call Gospel Haymanot: what might it mean to articulate the Gospel in a way that includes what we might call a theology of survival and flourishing? How do we contend with human oppression (especially when Christians have been complicit) and present a holistic faith that speaks to the private and public, internal and external? These and other questions are part of a vista that is open before us, and if the evangelical tradition is truly a biblical approach to the faith, it should be leading the way in answering these vital questions. To do this likely requires drawing on the integrated faith that is both explicit and latent in the Gospelist tradition of the Black church.

A closing question: Can evangelical theology convey good news for everyone? Yes, especially if we claim and steward the tradition, especially by bringing in the contributions of those Black Christians whose beliefs are evangelical even if they do not identify with the label. If we do this, we will help the evangelical tradition to live up to "the evangel" that has come to us in Christ.

BIBLIOGRAPHY

Bacote, Vincent. "Gifts from 'Father Abraham.'" *Comment* (Aug. 1, 2005): 12-13.

———. "Vincent Bacote: 'Critical thinking is obeying the commandment of loving your neighbor as yourself,'" interviewed by Bart Noort, accessed February 12, 2020,

Bratt, James D. *Abraham Kuyper: Modern Calvinist, Christian Democrat*. Grand Rapids: Wm. B. Eerdmans Publishing Co., 2013.

Camacho, Daniel José. "Common Grace and Race," *Reformed Journal*, January 10, 2015. https://reformedjournal.com/common-grace-and-race/.

Kuyper, Abraham. *Lectures on Calvinism*. Grand Rapids, MI: Eerdmans, 1931.

Steve McQueen, "Director's Cut: Steve McQueen (12 Years a Slave)," interview by Calum Marsh, *MTV.com*, October 16, 2013, http://www.mtv.com/news/2771146/12-years-a-slave-steve-mcqueen-interview/.

7

FROM HISTORICAL TRAUMA TO SHALOM

JACQUELINE T. DYER

The Black church is a reflection of the impact of trauma visited upon a people because of the paths through which The People must pass to get to God. That "The People"[259] survived characterizes God's relentless will to see His people healed and restored, especially to a right relationship with Him. However, like our 'now and not yet' soteriological understanding, both the resilience and the restoration exist and are yet unfolding. One reason for this is the impact of trauma visited upon The People. A lot has been realized in our healing from the trauma that has scarred us, but the work is not finished. God is moving us toward true shalom in Him despite our ongoing struggles with the unrest in our souls. Much contributes to that unrest; but the constant thread of historical and current trauma, and its threat through ongoing racism is the thread upon which I will tug. I will then discuss the need to recognize our unexpressed and, at times, disenfranchised grief and loss. The discussion will then turn to exploring lament as a culturally and theologically sound way to healthily vent. Finally, I will address how all this moves toward shalom. Each section of the chapter represents both individual and collective movement—in time, in culture, and in God. With lament as the conduit, this movement flows from the grief and loss of historical trauma by way of the lament towards shalom; a movement essential to liberation and to Gospel Haymanot.

Trauma and Historical Trauma

Trauma has a layered framework in that it is both historical and ongoing. Trauma itself has been most simply defined as an event that overwhelms someone's ability to cope.[260] It can result from incidents occurring on the spectrum from natural to man-made and can be cumulative. Symptoms may emerge over time and may include psychological/emotional, behavioral and physical manifestations.[261] The social nature of trauma can be relational, as between victim and perpetrator, or communal when others are involved. The involvement of others may, at times, be as witness to the situation.[262] Communal trauma may include entire groups where, for example, one group may perpetrate traumatic onslaughts toward one or more other groups. Regardless of the social level at which the traumatic incident occurs, relational or communal, it may be passed on from one generation to the next. The wounds and related responses become unintentionally and intentionally ingrained in the cultural memory of the affected groups. This occurs through the telling and retelling of past experiences, as well as through observed responses to those stories. It is this passing on of the traumatic event and the memory of it, along with the responses to and the remaining impact of the trauma that make it historical trauma.

When considering people of the ALANA ethnicities[263] in the United States, each of these groups have had historical trauma visited upon them at the inception of their interactions with the dominant culture. It is important to recognize that historical trauma in relation to people of color in the U.S. begins at first contact, which initiates the pathways of historical trauma. My focus will be on the historical and current trauma of African Americans. However, the themes evident in first contact practices can, with only minor changes, be overlaid upon the tactics consistently employed during European historical imperialism and colonization.[264] This expansionist mentality capitalized upon a conscripted Christian faith for validity.

> As Christianity came to be severed from its Jewish roots, it was remade into the cultural property of the West, the religious basis for justifying the colonial conquest that took off in the fifteenth century with the Portuguese and the Spanish, and that reached a zenith both in performance and in intellectual theorization as colonial and intellectual power shifted to France, England, and Germany beginning in the sixteenth century and culminating in the nineteenth century. Remade into cultural and political property and converted into an ideological instrument to aid and abet colonial conquest.[265]

Their goal of moving into new global territories was to establish and expand upon what they owned. Doing so resulted in exporting European cultures and languages. They also imported attitudes of superiority over and against people groups deemed lacking the same socio- economic markers preferred by the

Europeans. Differences were explained as deficits that required educations and governances, however patronizing.

Where the invaded cultural context did not match that of the invader, efforts were frequently implemented to change the existing culture. Intended benevolence may, at times, have given way to military impositions driven by greed, especially if the land itself or its rich resources were coveted by the invaders. Interestingly, the processes of imperialism and colonization appear to be similar to the spread of unchecked cancer in the body, wreaking destruction as they spread. This kind of incursion from its inception and origins in history is traumatizing. First contact set the pattern of interaction. Everything unfolding after that became tainted with the assumptions and prejudices inherent in the disdain that humans can generate toward each other. What then ensues is an often-automatic process of turning these patterns and perspectives into new norms. Those norms become—in relation to the offended people—racism.

Racism manifests societally as systemic, structural, and institutional. It is systemic via the automatic assumptions of advantages or inequalities woven into the societal perspectives that respectively benefit or harm depending upon whether a person belongs to the dominant or non- dominant group. [266] It becomes structural when the racist inequalities are embedded into all aspects of societal norms. When those inequities infiltrate and undergird policies and practices in any societal regulating body, it is institutional. Racism conjures a burden, like an evoked malevolence that afflicts those against whom it has been conjured, this also backfires upon those who conjure it.

Racism is behavior that privileges one group above another, where the privileged group has the power to establish and perpetuate its own privilege and discriminatory practices against the 'other,' whoever the other may be. The context of 'othering' is dependent upon the dominant culture, which contextualizes the norms, while any group different from that main culture falls into the category of 'other.' This is the first dehumanizing act. Subsequent acts follow as racism is ultimately incorporated into all structures and levels of society. It can be created or conjured individually or corporately, with intentional or unintentional actions.[267] Racism is complex, adaptive, and is frequently disowned by, yet remains embodied in, its conjurers.

This specter exists beneath their surfaces. Moreover, it distorts visual and cognitive perceptions of difference, creating a form of madness that damages its hosts with impetuses to engage in continued acts of dehumanization. Racism fluidly responds to context by becoming more subtle or overt depending upon whether racist practices are publicly condoned that year. When it is subtle, it can be difficult to identify. The persistent torment of racism makes it difficult to leave events of the past solely in history: "The repetitive nature of the incidents can make the experience traumatic…One incident alone may not be traumatizing, but multiple microaggressions can build to create an intense traumatic impact."[268] As such, ideas like "time heals all wounds" are basically nullified. Instead, reminders and re-enactments of historical harms cause the residual hurts of the past to remain close in the present.

Grief and Loss

If there is a traumatic incident, then there is a response. In some ways, the response to trauma includes a resistance to it. The response may be physical, psychological/emotional, or cognitive, whether at the individual or collective levels. Examples of this can be identified in the African-American resistance to slavery: "The slaves found ways to defend and protect themselves at the same time that they engaged and selectively embraced the more 'race neutral' aspects of European-American culture."[269] However while the responses included intentional resistance, it also included grief.

At the time of any historically traumatic event, something is lost. The grief which ensues and becomes transmitted may be marginalized or disenfranchised in many ways by both the perpetrating group and those who suffered. Historically, slaves did not draw attention to themselves, because any positive or negative attention might have resulted in increased suffering. Positive attention could yield increased work due to slave efficiency or rape if beauty was acknowledged. The negative attention could result in anything from a beating or being sold away from loved ones to death:

> It was during the daylight hours that each slave might be brought to his or her breaking point, that family members might be sold or exchanged, that children might be forced prematurely into adult work roles, that calculated or whimsical displays of violence might be heaped on the slaves—men, women, and children alike. The evening held its moments of sexual terror for black women, as it was commonplace for the owner, his sons, or his white employees to sexually savage black women.[270]

In these contexts, slaves would learn to give expression to their suffering away from potentially dangerous witnesses. These modes of protection became engrained into collective Black culture and were transmitted to later generations. They included messages that were ultimately seared into the backs of slaves and later passed on through the generations, communicating that if you could not bear the hardships of slave life, then your life would not last long.

I am Jamaican by birth and an immigrant to the U.S., but I have noted similarities in the cultural dynamics with Black American culture. One of the overlaps in the generationally transmitted rules related to enduring hardships is about what kinds of pain can be displayed and which should be borne in silence or solitude. My own grandmother, who lived through twelve pregnancies, including three still-born births and two infant deaths, was not known by any of her adult children to have shed tears or cried in their presence at any time. There was pride in those stories about her stoicism in the face of hardship, attributed to her as strength, during family reminiscences. This kind of older generation strength was sometimes contrasted against the failings of the "soft" younger generations to meet the same standard.

In the Black church, spaces to grieve are more readily provided when there are obvious reasons to grieve, such as a death or destruction. This is due, in part, to the overlay of the dominant cultural context, which equates pain with weakness or a kind of moral inadequacy or ineptitude. Our communal observations inform us, for instance, that one bears difficulties or suffering with the modeled grace of Coretta Scott King at the funeral of her husband, Martin Luther King, Jr. However, it is more firmly grounded in the cultural messages of pride in one's strength to bear up "through it all." The very faith of Black Americans is a testament to bearing "through it all" so that we can remain focused on what counts.

Generations have struggled through internalized images of a white Christ to get to a Black Jesus. I agree with Jacquelyn Grant that The People found their own ways to connect authentically to their God despite dominant cultural rhetoric and imagery.[271] They do so on an intuitive level because it is hard to tell your troubles to one who is aligned with and who looks like those who have oppressed and grieved you. Anecdotally, I have found that Black people tend to say they do not think of Jesus as having a color. This may be a result of being inundated since childhood with reliquary images in church buildings now utilized by The People, filled with paintings of Jesus in European depictions. Sometimes their homes would display the common-art images of a blond, blue-eyed God, far removed from His origins and the Gospel Haymanot context.

There is an internal resistance to thinking about Jesus and color because of those latent mental images. These same people also realize the fact that Jesus was hidden in Egypt for roughly 10 years when he was a child, based on the history documented in the Bible. Jesus—and his parents with him—had to have been dark-skinned to have been hidden in the African nation of Egypt. At best, there was a mixture of skin tones, but in that region of the world a blond haired, blue-eyed target would have been easy to find and kill. His image was re-appropriated by those who came and took other things as well. I dare say that if His image was not able to be adapted, there would have been a greater emphasis on adhering to the faith restrictions against images of God.

Resisting a misappropriated faith to find the true heart of it for themselves has been a mark of resilience for The People, and an appropriate response within the Gospel Haymanot tradition.

> [T]he languages and practices of dark people, most especially when they seek to comport themselves as

Christians in the world, must be engaged precisely in their theological specificity: that is, as ways of narrating being beyond race....Their effort—sometimes successful, other times not; sometimes consciously speaking in a Christian idiom, other times not… calls attention to the need to rend theology from the hands of whiteness rather than concede theology to whiteness.[272]

Resilience through resistance takes many forms for us. One of the healthiest manifestations of this combination of resilience and resistance facilitates expressing even the most disenfranchised grief. That pathway for all, for the present pain that lingers from the grief and loss of centuries past, is the lament.

Lament

The People have found ways to resist aspects of imposed dehumanization, even those which have crept into our cultures. The lament, in this context, becomes several things. It is a form of resistance and that makes it a form of resilience. It is also a pathway for releasing all forms of pain regardless of whether that pain is individual or collective or might not have otherwise been considered permissible for public consumption. When we sing or participate in what I will refer to as the "act of song," the barriers to grieving are released and all pain is permitted expression. That "act of song" is the way in which whether all are singing, as in a congregational hymn or a sing-along, or whether all are observing one sing, there is a collective participation in the song. The words express the known or unknown pain of many, and though the particular pain of one may be internally distinct from that of another, there is communal recognition that it exists and in this space the grief will not be denied.

> Feeling and the intentional action of being present are essential to the process of lamenting...As we feel our brokenness, our heartache, and—even as Jeremiah expressed—the inability to control our bowels, we remember God as our creator, defender, sustainer, and the supplier of our daily bread. It is in our weakest state that we learn best how to trust in the One who is able to keep us from stumbling and present us blameless before the presence of his glory with great joy.[273]

Among The People, whether in the Black church or in our communities at-large, music is a pathway for the cry within the soul. It carries the threads of present and centuries-old pain, directed to God the Father-Son-Holy Spirit. This pain is recognized in the song that provides the pathway for its expression. At times the expression is in the words of a hymn:

> I love the Lord; He heard my cries, and pitied every groan;
> Long as I live, and troubles rise, I'll hasten to His throne.[274]

This hymn, which emerged out of the pain of slaves, and its power to express the soul's anguish remains uncorrupted by time. Other times, expression lives in the passion behind the song. Take for instance, "A Change Is Gonna Come":

> Then I go to my brother
> And I say brother help me please
> But he winds up knockin' me

Back down on my knees, oh
There have been times that I thought I couldn't
last for long
But now I think I'm able to carry on
It's been a long, a long time coming
But I know a change is gonna come, oh yes it will ²⁷⁵

I refer to an unspoken pain at having progress unexpectedly and intentionally torn from attainment, yet also expresses a determined hope for change. This kind of dual recognition is not always conscious but seems to be always present in the ways that The People do song together. It can be found in secular music, as with the aforementioned song. However, much of secular Black music is undeniably rooted in the Black church. It is there where the collective 'act of song' seems more prevalent, because that is the place where song, laced with deeper and multiple meanings, was most frequently expressed. Through song, healing is facilitated for each according to the need:

> The gift of congregational or communal singing is often misunderstood and undervalued because of the singular focus on the aesthetic value of singing; yet the vital aspect of congregational or communal singing is the unification of the many into one collective voice. When many hearts, souls, and voices are aggregated in that fashion, the pain of the few becomes the pain of the many and, simultaneously, the hope of the few becomes the hope of the many. The kinesthetic action of breathing together merges with the theological reflection of the text that offers shared practice and creates a transition from the individual to the collective in breath, in voice and in power.

> Here solitude and loneliness give way to the temporal empowerment of togetherness—a powerful encounter that brings healing without minimizing one's personal experience.[276]

Perhaps this communal wisdom is why we often find in the Black church, that the solo singer, however imperfect, will be encouraged to continue the song and not be discouraged or give up.

Lament enables us to release even the wordless cry of the unspoken desolation covering over us to get to hope underneath. It may appear messy or sad, being threaded with grief, but lament is the ultimate expression of hope. When we cry out, we do so to the One more powerful than ourselves. We speak to God through our cries and groans, which become our prayer: "We do not know what we ought to pray for, but the Spirit himself intercedes for us through wordless groans. And he who searches our hearts knows the mind of the Spirit, because the Spirit intercedes for God's people in accordance with the will of God."[277] When we do not have the words, we trust that the Spirit knows what to say, and when we need permission to release all that pain, we look to our Bible and find models in the situations, the people, and verses throughout the Old and New Testaments. No matter how desperate the cause or how long the hurt has remained, when we pour it out to God: "Why, my soul, are you downcast? Why so disturbed within me? Put your hope in God,"[278] releasing the agony is, in itself, an act of faith.

Even when we involve others, and move from isolation to community, much of the discourse is still ultimately aimed toward God.

Shalom

> As the deer pants for streams of water, so my soul pants for you, my God.
> My soul thirsts for God, for the living God. When can I go and meet with God?
> My soul is downcast within me; therefore I will remember you....
> Deep calls to deep in the roar of your waterfalls; all your waves and breakers have swept over me.
> By day the LORD directs his love, at night his song is with me—a prayer to the God of my life.[279]

Our hope in God, despite what we see, feel, or encounter is what drives our ultimate motion. It is always toward God. Like a disrupted system beginning its return to equilibrium, we are moved to grieve losses resulting from our traumatic history and frequently from our traumatic present. Our grief moves us to seek release through faith-laced lament. The disturbance gets articulated. All this movement flows toward shalom because it stems from an unshakable hope in God's ability to transform what we cannot. Shalom encompasses flourishing yet can be interpreted to mean several things including peace, completeness, or well-being.[280] In relation to the movement from historical trauma to shalom, shalom can also include post-traumatic growth.

As noted when we opened this discussion about such movement, it is both now and not yet. Much of the historical trauma was predicated upon systemic, structural, and institutional racism, and much has been done to address it. This has helped to mitigate some of its impact upon the broader community. However, the work is not done. A more overt and visceral racism is re-emerging from the half-shadows into which it was consigned. Post the 2016 presidential election, there has been an almost rabid response to the prior Black occupation of the white house. The ease of that re-emergence, condoned in many ways by the 45th president, only supports the realization that the real work needed to eradicate racism, especially in this country, is yet to unfold. The malevolent specter has not yet been exorcised.

However, that context exists within the framework of a reality dominated by the omnipotent, Tripartite God. God is working His will toward the full deliverance of His People. We exist in a state where prior conditions have long been removed, yet we are not where we should be. That will take some time and effort on our part and God uses both time and people to work His will. Hope is not in vain, nor will it be frustrated much longer. However, we do not determine the moment of final salvation.

> For my thoughts are not your thoughts, neither are your ways my ways, declares the LORD. As the heavens are higher than the earth, so are my ways higher than your ways and my thoughts than your thoughts. As the rain and the snow come down from heaven, and do not return to it without watering the earth and making it bud and flourish, so that it yields seed for the sower and bread for the eater, so is my word that goes out from my mouth: It will not return to me empty, but will accomplish what I desire and achieve the purpose for which I sent it.[281]

We trust. And along with the author of the psalm, we yearn to be with God. We also know, whatever soul-deep disturbances may come, hope in God remains.

BIBLIOGRAPHY

Apache Indian Language. 1998-2015. Retrieved 6/5/2019, 2019, from http://www.native-languages.org/apache.

Ashenberg Straussner, Shulamith Lala and Alexandrea Josephine Calnan. "Trauma through the Life Cycle: A Review of Current Literature." In *Clinical Social Work* 42 (2014): 323- 335.

Bloom, Sandra L. "Every Time History Repeats Itself, the Price Goes Up: The Social Reenactment of Trauma." In *Sexual Addiction & Compulsivity* 3.3 (1996): 161-194, https://doi.org/10.1080/10720169608400111

Briere, John N. and Catherine Scott. *Principles of Trauma Therapy: A Guide to Symptoms, Evaluation, and Treatment (DSM-5 Update)*, 2nd ed. Thousand Oaks, CA: Sage Publications, 2015.

Bryant-Davis, Thema and Carlota Ocampo. "The Trauma of Racism: Implications for Counseling, Research, and Education." In *The Counseling Psychologist* 33 (2005): 574- 578.

Carter, J. Kameron. *Race: A Theological Account*. New York, NY: Oxford University Press, 2008.

Cooke, Sam. "A Change is Gonna Come," No. B1 in *Ain't That Good News*, RCA Victor: February 18, 1964, vinyl.

Cross, Jr. William E. "Black Psychological Functioning and the Legacy of Slavery: Myths and Realities." In *International Handbook of Multigenerational Legacies of Trauma*, ed. Y. Danieli, 387-400. New York, NY: Plenum Press, 1998.

Danzer, Graham. "White Psychologists and African Americans' Historical Trauma: Implications for Practice." In *Journal of Aggression, Maltreatment & Trauma* 25 (2016): 351-370, https://doi.org/10.1080/10926771.2016.1153550.

Gingrich, Heather Davediuk and Fred C Gingrich, *Treating Trauma in Christian Counseling*. Downers Grove, Illinois: InterVarsity Press, 2017.

Grant, Jacquelyn. *White Women's Christ and Black Women's Jesus: Feminist Christology and Womanist Response*. Atlanta, GA: American Academy of Religion, 1989.

Kanter, Jonathan. "A Preliminary Report on the Relationship Between Microaggressions Against Black People and Racism Among White College Students." In *Race and Social Problems* 9.4 (2017): 291-99, https://doi.org/10.1007/s12552-017-9214-0.

Mohatt, Nathaniel V. "Historical Trauma as Public Narrative: A Conceptual Review of How History Impacts Present-Day Health." In *Social Science & Medicine* 106 (April 2014): 128-136, http://dx.doi.org/10.1016/j.socscimed.2014.01.043.

Price, Emmett G. "There is a Balm in Gilead: A Call to Lament Together." In *A Time for Sorrow: Recovering the Practice of Lament in the Life of the Church*, eds. Scott Harrower and Sean M. McDonough, 89-100. Peabody, MA: Hendrickson Publishers, 2019.

Salter, Phia S., Glenn Adams, and Michael J. Perez. "Racism in the Structure of Everyday Worlds: A Cultural-Psychological Perspective." In *Current Directions in Psychological Science* 27.3, 150-155 (June 2018), http://doi.org/10.1177/0963721417724239.

Smallwood, Richard. "I Love the Lord," No. A3 in *Give Us Peace: Richard Smallwood & Union Temple Young Adult Choir*, Gerald Lewis Recording: August 25, 1976, vinyl.

Utsey, Shawn O. "Cultural, Sociofamilial, And Psychological Resources That Inhibit Psychological Distress in African Americans Exposed to Stressful Life Events and Race- Related Stress." In *Journal of Counseling Psychology* 55.1 (2008): 49-62, https://www.researchgate.net/publication/224071411_Cultural_Sociofamilial_and_Psychological_Resources_That_Inhibit_Psychological_Distress_in_African_Americans_Exposed_to_Stressful_Life_Events_and_Race-Related_Stress

_____. Joseph G. Ponterotto, and Jerlym S. Porter. "Prejudice and Racism, Year 2008-Still Going Strong: Research on Reducing Prejudice With Recommended Methodological Advances." In *Journal of Counseling and Development* 86.3 (2008): 339-347.

CONCLUSION:
A Living Haymanot of the Whole Gospel

VINCE L. BANTU

The Gospel is a beacon of victory that has been signaled since humanity's banishment from Eden, was fully realized in the Resurrection of Jesus Christ, and has been a force of empowerment to believers for centuries. The Gospel has been the single greatest impetus for Black identity, creativity, and social organization since our inception as a people. The beauty and nobility of Blackness is affirmed in Holy Scripture. Indeed, Black skin is the only skin color group that is specifically highlighted in Scripture! In contrast to surrounding ancient Near Eastern civilizations that caricaturized Black Africans, the Bible speaks of Black people as "tall and smooth-skinned" and that Black is beautiful, a thing not to be disparaged.[282] God even rebukes Miriam for her denigration of Moses' Cushite wife and ironically punishes Miriam with an affliction that turns her skin white.[283] Throughout the development of Black theology, the Gospel has continued to imbue African believers with a sense of being made in the image of the Creator. In her *Hymn to Humanity*, Phillis

Wheatley comments on the implications of the Incarnation for the human condition:

> Descent to earth, there place thy throne;
> To succor man's afflicted son
> Each human heart inspire:
> To act in bounties unconfin'd,
> Enlarge the closed contracted mind,
> And fill it with thy fire.[284]

In a manner typical to her literary corpus, Wheatley's unbridled optimism regarding the human experience is grounded in the hope of Christ's saving work on earth. Like all Americans of African descent during this time period, Wheatley intimately understood human suffering and experienced one of the vilest examples of state-sanctioned oppression in human history. As Day has pointed out in her chapter, the Gospel has been the foundation of the greatest moments in Black history in the U.S. Despite the perversion of Christian theology that was deployed in support of American slavery, Wheatley's hope for humanity was grounded in the appearance of God in Christ. For Wheatley—as well as countless Black Christian slaves—the Gospel was all the more "good news" in the midst of intense suffering. The victory of God was present.

Wheatley's prose demonstrates how, for slave Christians, the Gospel was good news for "afflicted" and "closed-minded" humanity. Rather than a humanistic optimism grounded in society's capability for benevolence, Wheatley grounded her aspirations in the assumption of the "throne" by the King Jesus. The reign of Christ on earth touches the entire person: hearts are "inspired," minds are "enlarged," and good deeds are "unconfined." Wheatley's theological vision conceived of no distinction between spiritual, physical, and social transformation—the Gospel touches each of these realms. J. Deotis Roberts connects the theological ingenuity of African-American slaves such as Wheatley to existing African visions of God:

> The traditional African conception of God is also monotheistic. The lesser spirits are God's ministers in relation to human beings. In many ways, this God resembles most the God of the Old Testament. When African slaves were introduced to the Bible, they were able to derive meanings from it that were hidden to the oppressors. They understood God against the background of traditional beliefs in a Supreme Being. They were aware of both the power and the moral uprightness of God. Jehovah, as described in the Old Testament, was a close facsimile of the African Supreme Being they had known. As they faced a situation of great hardship, the liberation of the Hebrews from Egyptian bondage caught their fancy. For the black oppressed, facing daily the white oppressors, the exodus took on a political as well as a religious meaning. They believed that something would happen in heaven and on earth when they sang, "Go down, Moses, 'way down in Egypt land; Tell ole Pharaoh, Let my people go!"[285]

Even as Robertson makes clear in his chapter in this volume, the Old Testament authors engaged and contextualized their predecessors in response to their changing situations. In the same way, Black Christians responded to the biblical text in unique ways shaped by our situation that resulted in one of the most impactful theological methodologies in Christian history.

As Roberts states: "No committed black church leader or scholar would wish to tone down his (James Cone's) liberation motif. Our people have endured and are enduring too much deep ethnic suffering for that. But the oppression-liberation formula does not adequately unlock the biblical message."[286] For Roberts, adequate biblical theology deals with good news for the entire person, indeed the entire society. Salvation is physical, social, and spiritual and can only be found in Christ as revealed in His holy Word. While Roberts critiques Liberation Theology for its omission of the biblical impulse towards reconciliation, he also points out the weaknesses of Western theology while uplifting the strengths of African-American faith: "Since the New Testament has been privatized, futurized, and eschatologized by Western scholars, the black perspective on the New Testament may save this part of the Scripture and in so doing save the church from spiritual and moral bankruptcy."[287] The beauty and power of the Gospel of Jesus Christ is that it does not need saving or defending when it is corrupted by imperial theology. For, as Edwards has illustrated, the New Testament presents the marginalized of society as the model Christian teachers. Therefore, we must continue to resist the tendency to measure the vitality of the Church by its most privileged members. To Roberts' point, from the times of the New Testament, the Gospel movement has been a grassroots community movement whose most crucial leadership has emerged from situations of terrible human suffering. People of privilege have always been invited into and included in the ministry of the Church following renunciations of systemic injustice and solidarity with the oppressed. The corruption of New Testament Christianity, to which Roberts refers, is a consistent outgrowth of what Harriet Jacobs called "Satan's church here below."[288] This should not, however, be seen as representative of the Body of Christ. God's people have at all times and places of Christian history represented the New Testament faith as described in Scripture. The Black theological articulation of the Gospel is one of many witnesses to biblical ecclesiology.

Throughout my early years of schooling, I felt as if leaving my Christian context in urban St. Louis for the world of theological academia was like a bird leaving the nest but falling into water. Perhaps the central reason why I was drowning instead of learning to fly was that the holistic faith I was raised in among African-American Christians in my community was not reflected in the theological paradigms that were being taught to me in systematic theology courses. Even though I got saved when I was a small child and was active in ministry and sharing the Gospel for years before coming to college, I had no idea what an "evangelical" was before going to a Christian college and majoring in theology. At first what was being described as "evangelical" sounded good—a Christian that is committed to the authority of Scripture and burdened to share the Good News to the lost.

However, as I became further acquainted with white, middle-class American evangelicalism, the full and inescapable definition of "evangelical" became untenable for me. The sustained and continued complicity with white supremacy and American nationalism coupled with a weak theology of justice made it clear for me why the term "evangelical" has never experienced much currency with the Black Church tradition. African-American and other allied students exhibiting a commitment to justice and reconciliation earned reputations as "Marxist," "socialist," and "liberal." I assumed I was a liberal if being "liberal" meant being radically committed to liberation for the oppressed. But when I moved on from evangelical institutions to mainline liberal academic institutions, I realized I was actually not a liberal.

While in evangelical contexts I was labeled a socialist, during my time in mainline academic institutions I was labelled a fundamentalist for my commitment to the authority of Scripture, Trinitarian orthodoxy, and the exclusive truth of the Gospel. Furthermore, what was being presented to me in mainline institutions as "Black theology" sounded wholly unfamiliar from anything I had ever heard in a Black church. While the commitment to Black dignity and flourishing espoused in Black liberation theology was a helpful corrective to the inundation of white supremacist evangelicalism I had experienced up to that point, the ambiguous or outright lack of commitment to the historic Christian faith that characterizes much of academic, liberation theology was problematic and alien to the lived theology of the Black church. The discontinuity of evangelicalism and the Black theology of mainline, liberal academia from the lived theology of the Black church prompted me to return to this theological tradition. The Black Christian witness to the harmony between justice and orthodoxy is a helpful corrective to the bifurcated theological expressions that characterize much of the academy. This Gospelist tradition, which has stood as a source of justice and righteousness among Black Christians, is rooted in the biblical vision of Christian community.

Gospel Haymanot Acted

The Book of Acts prescribes better than any other early Christian text God's vision for His Church on earth. At His ascension back to the Father's right hand, Jesus told His disciples that "you will be my witnesses in Jerusalem, and in all Judea and Samaria and to the ends of the earth."[289] This commission is a fitting prolegomenon to the world's first Church History as this tripartite structure describes the Apostle's mission work focusing on these three regions successively. Before narrating Paul's mission to the "ends of the earth" or Peter's work in Judea and Samaria, the opening chapters of Acts tells of the initial apostolic work in Jerusalem. In these foundational chapters, the fundamental nature of the Church is modeled after the earthly ministry of Christ as a model for God's people. The nature of the Church's work in society and its subsequent witness to the political systems of the world are encapsulated wonderfully in Acts 5:12-42. The public ministry of the Church in the fifth chapter of Acts vividly portrays the Gospel in ways that have been lived out by Black Christians and countless others. Acts 5 serves as an illustration for Gospel proclamation in four distinct ways: Empowerment, Resistance, Orthodoxy, and Solidarity.

Empowerment:

The prophet Isaiah relayed the Lord's rhetorical question to His people regarding proper worship: "Is not this the kind of fasting I have chosen: to loose the chains of injustice and untie the cords of the yoke, to set the oppressed free and break every yoke?"[290] In the same way that the Apostle and brother of our Lord Jesus explained that "faith without works is dead,"[291] the Old Testament prophets clarified that worship is empty when unaccompanied with social justice. Acts 5:12-16 sets the stage for the Apostle's second encounter with the Sanhedrin by describing their ministry of healing outside of the temple in Jerusalem. The Sadducees brought the Apostles to court due to their jealousy (5:17) because of the increasing number of Christians (5:14) who were flocking to the Apostles due to the miraculous signs (5:12) and healings (5:15-16) that were occurring. The empowerment of the poor, oppressed, and sick was an integral component of the early Jerusalem Church.

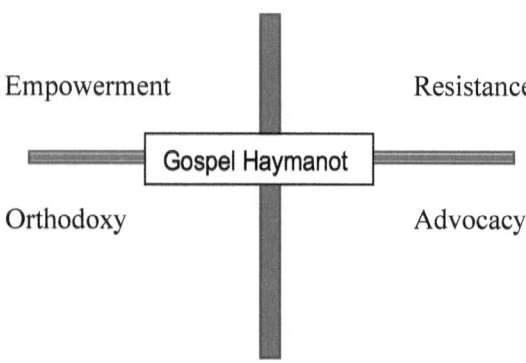

The believers shared food regularly, sold property, submitted resources to the Church, and empowered the poor to the point that both poverty and the concept of personal property were non-existent in their community (2:45-46; 4:32-37). Throughout much of conservative, evangelical Christianity, commitment to empowering the poor and oppressed has been treated as an elective or a specified calling rather than a mark of any orthodox Christian community. In many of those same circles, the assertion that prayer, worship, or discipleship are specified callings that are not universal to all Christians would appear ludicrous. In the same way, the call to end poverty is upon all of God's people in all times and places. To remove community development from the ministry of the Church is to alter the fundamental nature of the good news for the poor (Lk. 4:18).

Resistance:

After a miraculous rescue from prison, the apostles were arrested again for continuing to proclaim the Gospel in the temple courts. When the members of the Sanhedrin proclaimed the legal boundaries against Christian proclamation and witness,

CONCLUSION:

the apostles responded: "We must obey God rather than human beings."[292] The statement of the Apostles' resolve is the answer to the mirror situation when Peter and John stood before the Sanhedrin previously under the same charges. When the chief priests and teachers of the law instructed the Apostles to refrain from teaching the Gospel, the apostles asked the rhetorical question: "Which is right in God's eyes: to listen to you, or to him? You be the judges! As for us, we cannot help (lit: "it is not possible for us") speaking about what we have seen and heard."[293] The earliest Christians understood that bearing witness to the Kingdom of God will put the Church at odds with earthly authorities. The contrast in 5:29 between the "first" or "higher persuasion" (*peitharxeo*), referring to God, and the simple reference of "humans" (*anthropois*) for the highest authority in Israel should not be underestimated. While God's people are forbidden from physical resistance of injustice (Rom. 13:5), the presence of darkness in earthly authorities (Jn.14:30) necessitates political, social, and theological resistance on the part of God's people in the face of evil (2 Cor. 10:4; Eph. 6:12).

Orthodoxy:

The apostles were brought to trial before the Sanhedrin under charges of "teaching in the name" of Jesus.[294] The public witness of the early believers was centered on a particular message—that Jesus Christ is Lord and the only path to human salvation. Peter and John followed their non-violent resistance to the Sanhedrin with an exposition of Trinitarian orthodoxy: God the Father raised Jesus with all power and authority to which the Holy Spirit testifies to the world (Acts 5:31-32). The charges brought against Peter and John were instigated by "an act of kindness" (Acts 4:9) involving healing a sick man as well as the Sanhedrin's aversion for the Christian Gospel. The promulgation of Christian theology enraged the authorities and the social justice work of the Christians "filled them with jealousy."[295] The theological and sociological aspects of Gospel witness are inseparable and indistinguishably put God's People at odds with power systems.

Contemporary theological systems that place appropriate emphasis on God's preferential option for the poor often stray from the exclusive source of liberation which is fully realized only in Jesus Christ. Theological exclusivity is a stumbling block in these communities. Virgilio Elizondo claimed that the way of Jesus cannot be described as exclusive: "the way of Jesus incorporated all the others, functioned through all of them, and went beyond them."[296] Indeed, the Bible makes clear that the People of God are composed of every nation tribe and tongue and exist for the liberation of the poor.[297] However, the way of Jesus also calls His People to an alternative lifestyle and theological worldview. The Gospel asserts claims about God, humanity, and salvation that are in direct contrast with religious and theological systems.[298] Often liberation theologians write from a reactionary standpoint, offering valid critiques to equally problematic evangelical attempts at over-spiritualizing the social implications in the Bible.

However, the necessity of exclusive faith in the Gospel message as revealed in Christ cannot and should never be equivocated with Western evangelical Christendom. Justice for the poor is a biblical agenda and was not invented by Marxism or socialism. In the same way, salvation by grace through faith in Christ alone is not an innovation of Western evangelicals.

These various theological trajectories have valid points to offer. As Bacote outlines in his chapter, we must avoid the extremes of denying the weaknesses or dismissing the strengths of these frameworks. The Gospel of Jesus Christ is the primary lens through which we must filter between the two. The Gospel witness in Acts displays the complex nature of the Gospel's exclusive supremacy and universal appeal. The apostles declared in their first encounter with the Sanhedrin that "salvation is found in no one else, for there is no other name under heaven given to humanity by which we must be saved."[299]

Advocacy:

In describing the theological significance of reconciliation, J. Deotis Roberts pushes dominant discourses in Black Theology by clarifying the end goal of the black struggle for liberation. Roberts claims that liberation and reconciliation are harmonious poles of the black theological project.[300] The spiritual danger of wealth should not lead to a villainization of the privileged nor should God's preferential option for the poor lead to a romanticization of the poor. All have sinned, require salvation, and have access to redemption through Christ—Black, white, rich, poor, male, or female. Yet God's covenant with us is realized in a chosen race that is comprised of every tribe, nation, and tongue. This is reflected in Rowe's reflection on peace studies and elevation of the South African concept of *ubuntu* ("a person is a person through other persons"). The seriousness with which God takes poverty and injustice warns against ignoring God's call for liberation. Simultaneously, the universality both of sin and God's love points the Church toward the beloved community. In the face of injustice, Peter and John found an advocate on the Sanhedrin in the person of Gamaliel. A teacher of the Apostle Paul, Gamliel spoke up in defense of the apostles and convinced the Sanhedrin not to put them to death.

Through his advocacy, Gamaliel used his platform to advocate for the oppressed and put his reputation on the line as he argued against popular opinion.[301]

The ministry of the Church has a special focus on the liberation of the poor and involves the partnership of believers in positions of power. Much of conservative Christianity treats participation in the work of justice and restoration as a matter of specialized calling. As Bacote explains in his chapter, evangelical theology has suffered from the tendency to excuse itself from participation in issues of injustice. The Acts account describes a community characterized by truth and justice, including many poor and some wealthy members. Joseph—or Barnabas—was a Levite who placed his wealth in the service of the Church, much like every privileged member of the early Church (Acts 4:36). Throughout Scripture, and especially in the Gospels, inclusion of the wealthy and privileged among God's People is always accompanied by acts of sacrifice, giving, and reparations (Lk. 19:1-10; Acts 16:11-15). Conversely, failure on the part of the privileged to answer Christ's call to submit their riches to His Kingdom rule is strongly condemned throughout Scripture (Matt. 6:24; 19:16-30; 1 Tim. 6:10; Heb. 13:5; Jas. 5:1-6). Participation in the work of justice is expected from God's People and assumed to be the Church's responsibility (2 Cor. 8:7).

The wholistic Gospel Haymanot of the earliest Church was multifaceted with a purview of good news for the physical, spiritual, social, and political realms of humanity. Gospel Haymanot comes from the Black spiritual tradition rooted in the Exodus narrative. As Robertson's chapter outlines, the Exodus themes—which are advanced by the Hebrew prophets centuries later—include: God raising up His messenger (resistance) to call for those in power to liberate His People (advocacy) which

God enacts through the plagues and a miraculous exodus (empowerment) so that He can establish His covenant code with His People (orthodoxy). The comprehensive ministry approach of Gospel-influenced Christian communities is expected to occur in the context of two interdependent realities: liberation and suffering.

Liberation & Suffering:

Much of liberal and liberation discourse on God is theologically bankrupt in their indistinguishability from secular humanism; the foundation and end goal of liberation is human dignity. Rowe offers a corrective to this in his discussion of the *imago sui*—the elevation of one's own group as the center of human existence. Too often, humanistic tendencies in theology elevate the oppressed group as the end goal of God's activity in the world. In the same way, much of conservative, evangelical theology is morally deficient in its compliance with systemic injustice under the guise of Christian piety. The biblical vision of God's salvation work among His People is characterized by a paradoxical symbiosis between suffering and liberation. Suffering without liberation is masochism; liberation without suffering is triumphalist, humanistic prosperity theology.

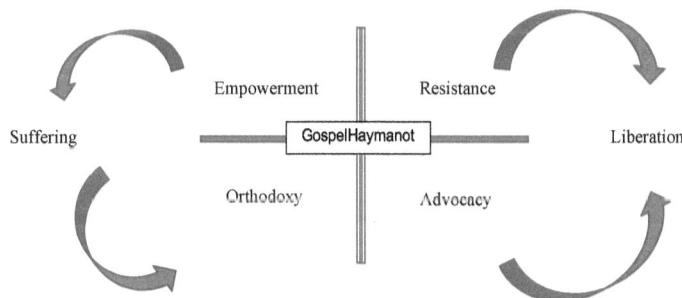

The narrative of Acts 5:12-42 vividly portrays the liberation-suffering cycle in which God leads His People. The cycle of oppression-liberation-suffering transpires twice in this single periscope: 1.) The apostles experienced persecution by being thrown in prison for preaching the lordship of Christ and for empowering the oppressed (Acts 5:17-18); the apostles are brought to court to stand trial for continuing the ministry of the Church (Acts 5:26-27); 2.) The apostles are freed from prison by an angel (Acts 5:19); the apostles are flogged but spared from death due to Gamaliel's advocacy (Acts 5:40); 3.) The angel commands the apostles to return back to the temple and continue ministering the Gospel (Acts 5:20); The apostles again continued to minister the Gospel throughout Jerusalem and counted their sufferings as blessing (Acts 5:41-42). The Black struggle for liberation in the twenty-first century finds voice in this passage: the persecution from which God liberates the apostles is an unjust judicial and incarceration system. The #blacklivesmatter movement stands in the African-American Gospelist tradition of freedom fighters entering into suffering in pursuit of liberation based on the premise that Black people are fearfully and wonderfully made in the image of God.

The evangelistic impulse of the Great Commission[302] compels God's People to enter into suffering for the salvation of the lost and oppressed. While the conditions of our earthly people are of great importance, Christians from particular communities are part of a larger Body of Christ for whose promulgation our liberation is purposed. As Edwards points out in his chapter, being "worthy of Gospel" as the Christian's highest allegiance was at the heart of the New Testament world. At the heart of the biblical narrative that has provided the foundation for Black Gospel Haymanot—the Exodus narrative—God's liberation of the Hebrews from slavery had an end goal that was greater than itself, the glory of God: "Let my people go, so that they may worship me."[303] In light of God's directive to pharaoh, the work of the Church in the world must assume the necessity and interdependence of the liberation of the oppressed with orthodox worship of the one, true God. The Lord set the apostles free multiple times in the opening chapters of Acts and then immediately calls them back into the fray of Gospel witness. The apostles provide a framework for the continuing ministry of God's Church to be obedient, submissive agents in His liberative victory over a world fraught with sin and injustice.

In His faithfulness, God has empowered the Black Church to respond to His good news with a vibrant, liberative, and comprehensive theological paradigm that has been the single greatest source of empowerment for our people. The perspectives offered in this volume represent theological framing of a lived theological tradition that reared and shaped the present scholars. The theological paradigm that has shaped Black ecclesial life and struggle for freedom provides the basis for the discourse method based in orthodoxy and justice which we call Gospel Haymanot. The power of God that has brought us a mighty long way and will bring us over to the Promised Land is the universal, liberative power of the Gospel.

BIBLIOGRAPHY

Elizondo, Virgilio. *Galilean Journey: The Mexican-American Promise*. Maryknoll, NY: Orbis Books, 1983.

Roberts, J. Deotis. *Black Theology in Dialogue*. Philadelphia, PA: The Westminster Press, 1987.

Rodney Steven Sadler Jr., Rodney Steven. *Can a Cushite Change His Skin? An Examination of Race, Ethnicity, and Othering in the Hebrew Bible*. New York, NY: T&T Clark, 2005.

AUTHOR BIOGRAPHIES

Vincent Bacote (Ph.D., Drew University) is an Associate Professor of Theology and the Director of the Center for Applied Christian Ethics at Wheaton College in Wheaton, IL. He is author of *The Political Disciple: A Theology of Public Life* (2015) and has numerous contributions to books, magazines, and journals. He lives in Glen Ellyn, IL with his family.

Vince L. Bantu is Assistant Professor of Church History and Black Church Studies at Fuller Theological Seminary in Houston, TX. Vince also serves as the Ohene (President) of Meachum School of Haymanot, an institution providing contextual theological education for the Black church and community. Vince is also the author of *A Multitude of All Peoples: Engaging Ancient Christianity's Global Identity* and is currently editing a reader of early African and Asian Christian texts with the University of California Press. Vince also serves as the Ohene (President) for the Society of Gospel Haymanot, an academic colloquium for Black faculty and students of religion and theology. Vince, his wife Diana, and their two daughters live in Houston, TX.

Jacqueline T. Dyer, PhD, MSW, MAUML, LICSW, is Assistant Professor of Counseling and Director of Counseling and

Academic Initiatives at Gordon Conwell Theological Seminary-Boston. There she teaches in the licensure track Master of Arts in Counseling Program and developed the Pastoral Care and Chaplaincy degree track. Her research and scholarly interests include clergy compassion fatigue, historical trauma, and domestic violence in faith communities. Dr. Dyer has served as a clinical supervisor in secular and Christian agencies, and as a volunteer facilitator for a Christian domestic violence support-group. Her volunteer time also included serving on the leadership team for Clergy Women United, part of the Black Ministerial Alliance of Greater Boston. Dr. Dyer accepted her call to ministry September 23rd, 2012. In May of 2016 she received her license to preach, and on September 30th, 2018, was ordained in the Baptist Denomination, both at her faith home, Peoples Baptist Church in Boston, where she is an Associate Minister and facilitates Spiritual Direction meetings.

Rev. Dr. Dennis R. Edwards is currently Associate Professor of New Testament at North Park Theological Seminary (Chicago, IL). He's the author of 1 Peter in the *Story of God Bible Commentary* series (Zondervan), *What is the Bible and How Do We Understand It?* (Herald Press), and *Might from the Margins: How the Gospel Turns the Tables on Injustice* (Herald Press). Dennis has been married to Susan Steele Edwards since 1982. They are the parents of four adult children, have two grandsons, and are expecting two more grandchildren. Dennis has over thirty years of urban pastoral ministry experience. He most recently served as senior pastor of The Sanctuary Covenant Church in Minneapolis, MN. Prior to that, he was the founding pastor of Peace Fellowship Church in Washington, DC; associate and then lead pastor of Washington Community Fellowship on

Capitol Hill; and founding pastor of New Community Church in Brooklyn, NY. Dennis holds a Bachelor of Science degree in chemical engineering (Cornell University) and has been a high school science and math teacher. He also earned a Master of Divinity degree in Urban Ministry (Trinity Evangelical Divinity School) as well as Master of Arts and PhD degrees in Biblical Studies (Catholic University of America). Dennis enjoys playing his flute and saxophone, as well as weightlifting, cycling, and playing racquetball as much as his body will let him.

Cleotha Robertson is an Assistant Professor of Old Testament at Alliance Theological Seminary in New York, NY (Ph.D., New York University; D.Min. Lutheran Theological Seminary). He is also a graduate of Dartmouth College (B.A.), Gordon-Conwell Theological Seminary (M.Div.), and Brooklyn College (M.Sc.). Cleotha Robertson is the Senior Pastor of Sound View Presbyterian Church in the Bronx, New York. He has served in this capacity since 1994.

Nicholas Rowe, Ph.D., is Dean of Student Engagement and Associate Professor of History and Peace Studies at Gordon College. Before this, he spent the past ten years on the faculty of St Augustine College of South Africa in Johannesburg, culminating in the role of Academic Dean and Interim President. His teaching and research interests include identity formation and how communities use the past to form their identities and how this fuels intergroup conflict. He also has more than twenty years consulting with communities about cross-racial and cross-ethnic reconciliation and pastoral counseling for reconciling communities in the USA and South Africa. His international experiences in higher education have convinced him that this is a strategic point in world history and that communities the world over require leaders who are lively in imagination, protective of the dignity of persons, relentless in pursuit of the common good, and attentive in spirit. He is married to Sheila Wise Rowe, a professional therapist. They have two adult children.

NOTES

1 C. Eric Lincoln & Lawrence H. Mamiya, *The Black Church in the African American Experience* (Durham, NC: Duke University Press, 1990).

2 Benjamin Barber, *Jihad vs. McWorld: Terrorism's Challenge to Democracy* (New York, NY: Ballantine Books, 1995), 5

3 Stacey Floyd-Thomas, Juan Floyd-Thomas, Carol B. Duncan, Stephen G. Ray, Jr. & Nancy Lynne Westfield, *Black Church Studies: An Introduction* (Nashville, TN: Abingdon Press, 2007), 105

4 William F. Arndt & F. Wilbur Gingrich, *A Greek-English Lexicon of the New Testament and Other Early Christian Literature: A Translation and Adaptation of the Fourth Revised and Augmented Edition of Walter Bauer's Griechisch-Deutsches Wörterbuch zu den Schriften des Neuen Testaments und der übrigen urchristlichen Literatur* (Chicago, IL: The University of Chicago Press, 1979), 798-802.

5 James H. Cone, *For My People: Black Theology and the Black Church* (Maryknoll, NY: Orbis Books, 1984), 70; Mercy Amba Oduyoye, *Introducing African Women's Theology* (Cleveland, OH: Pilgrim Press/The United Church Press, 2001), 27.

6 Wolf Leslau, *Comparative Dictionary of Ge'ez* (Wiesbaden: Harrassowitz Verlag, 2006), 221.

7   A genre of theological literature unique to the Ethiopian Christian tradition, often translated as "theological treatise," "commentary," "dissertation," or "homily."

8   Zar'a Ya'qob, *The Homily of Zär 'a Ya 'əqob's* Mäṣḥafa Bərhan *on the Rite of Baptism and Religious Instruction*, ed. Getatchew Haile (Louvain: Secretariat du SCO, 2013), 81.

9   Giyorgis of Segla, *Maṣḥafa Mesṭir*, ed. Yaqob Beyene (Louvain: Secretariat du SCO, 1990), 128.

10 *The Ge'ez Acts of Abba Ǝsṭifanos of G^{w}endag^{w}ende*, ed. Getatchew Haile (Louvain: Secretariat du SCO, 2006), 1.

11 David Moberg, *The Great Reversal: Reconciling Evangelism and Social Concern*, 2nd ed. (Eugene, OR: Wipf & Stock, 2006), 16.

12 George M. Marsden, *Fundamentalism and American Culture*, 2nd ed. (Oxford: Oxford University Press, 2006), 36-37.

13 Michael O. Emerson & Christian Smith, *Divided by Faith: Evangelical Religion and the Problem of Race in America* (Oxford: Oxford University Press, 2000), 55-56.

14 Arthur H. Fauset, *Black Gods of the Metropolis: Negro Religious Cults of the Urban North* (Philadelphia, PA: University of Pennsylvania Press, 1944), 10.

15 Fauset, *Black Gods*, 121.

16 Edward E. Curtis IV & Danielle Brune Sigler, *The New Black Gods: Arthur Huff Fauset and the Study of African American Religions* (Bloomington, IN: Indiana University Press, 2009), 7.

17 Albert B. Cleage, Jr., *Black Christian Nationalism: New Directions for the Black Church* (Detroit, MI: Luxor Publishers, 1987), 9.

18 E. Franklin Frazier, "The Negro Church and Assimilation," in *African-American Religious Thought: An Anthology*, eds. Cornel West & Eddie S. Glaude, Jr., 62-73 (Louisville, KY: Westminster John Knox, 2003), 65-66; while Frazier's claim that emancipation

cripped black family networks has been criticized, his correlation of the vitality of the black church and black community has been largely accepted, Marla F. Frederick, *Between Sundays: Black Women and Everyday Struggles of Faith* (Berkeley, CA: University of California Press, 2003), 86.

19   James H. Cone, *Black Theology and Black Power*, 7th ed. (Maryknoll, NY: Orbis Books, 2005), 36.

20   James H. Cone, *God of the Oppressed* (Maryknoll, NY: Orbis Books, 1975), 9.

21   Gustavo Gutiérrez, *A Theology of Liberation: History, Politics, and Salvation*, 2nd ed. (Maryknoll, NY: Orbis Books, 1988), 85.

22   James H. Cone, *The Cross and the Lynching Tree* (Maryknoll, NY: Orbis Books, 2011), 3.

23   Delores S. Williams, *Sisters in the Wilderness: The Challenge of Womanist God-Talk* (Maryknoll, NY: Orbis Books, 1993), 3.

24   Gutiérrez, *A Theology of Liberation*, 85.

25   Cone, *Black Theology*, 85.

26   Anthony B. Bradley, *Liberating Black Theology: The Bible and the Black Experience in America* (Wheaton, IL: Crossway Books, 2010), 92. A more gracious treatment of Liberation Theology is found in Thabityi M. Anyabwile, *The Decline of African-American Theology: From Biblical Faith to Cultural Captivity* (Downers Grove, IL: InterVarsity Press, 2007). However, Anyabwile falls prey to the same tendency as Bradley in defining orthodoxy according to Eurocentric expressions of theology, 175.

27   Cone, *Black Theology*, 114.

28   Cone, *For My People*, 101-2.

29   James H. Cone, *For My People: Black Theology and the Black Church* (Maryknoll, NY: Orbis Books, 1984), 53.

30   Cone, *Black Theology*, xii.

31   Gutiérrez, *A Theology of Liberation*, 84-85.

32   Williams, *Sisters in the Wilderness*, 4.

33   Jacquelyn Grant, *White Women's Christ and Black Women's Jesus: Feminist Christology and Womanist Response*. (Oxford: The American Academy of Religion, 1989)., 212.

34   Carl F. Ellis, Jr., *Free at Last? The Gospel in the African-American Experience*, 2nd ed. (Downers Grove, IL: InterVarsity Press, 1996), 118.

35   Kelly Brown Douglas, *Stand Your Ground: Black Bodies and the Justice of God* (Maryknoll, NY: Orbis Books, 2015), 139.

36   Nicholas P. Wolterstorff, *Journey Toward Justice: Personal Encounters in the Global South* (Grand Rapids, MI: Baker Academic, 2013), 98.

37   D.H. Dilbeck, *Frederick Douglass: America's Prophet* (Chapel Hill, NC: University of North Carolina Press, 2018), 2.

38   Bryan Stevenson, *Just Mercy: A Story of Justice and Redemption* (New York, NY: Spiegel & Grau, 2014); Michelle Alexander, *The New Jim Crow: Mass Incarceration in the Age of Colorblindness* (New York, NY: The New Press, 2010); Dominique Gilliard, *Rethinking Incarceration: Advocating for Justice that Restores* (Downers Grove, IL: InterVarsity Press, 2018).

39   Brown Douglas, *Stand Your Ground*, 138.

40   Ellis, *Free at Last?*, 30.

41   J. Deotis Roberts, *Liberation and Reconciliation*, 2nd ed. (Louisville, KY: Westminster John Knox Press, 2005), 4.

42   Arthur Huff Fauset, *Black Gods of the Metropolis: Negro Religious Cults of the Urban North* (Philadelphia, PA: University of Pennsylvania Press, 1944), 2. However, there was a significant population of Kongolese slaves brought to the Caribbean that had been Catholics due to Portuguese mission efforts since the fifteenth century. These Kongolese Catholic slaves in the Caribbean are attested in various white sources during the seventeenth and eighteenth centuries, Jeroen Dewulf, *The Pinkster King and the*

King of Kongo: The Forgotten History of America's Dutch-Owned Slaves (Jackson, MS: University Press of Mississippi, 2017), 125.

43   Katharine Gerbner, *Christian Slavery: Conversion and Race in the Protestant Atlantic World* (Philadelphia, PA: University of Pennsylvania Press, 2018), 194.

44   Fauset, *Black Gods*, 6.

45   Mark K. Smith, *Stono: Documenting and Interpreting a Southern Slave Revolt* (Columbia, SC: University of South Carolina Press, 2005), 14.

46   Smith, *Stono*, 14

47   Galawdewos, *Gadla Walatta Petros*, ed. Wendy Laura Belcher & Michael Kleiner, in *The Life and Struggles of Our Mother Walatta Petros* (Princeton, NJ: Princeton University Press, 2015), 119-124.

48   Frederick, *Between Sundays*, 4.

49   Phillis Wheatley, "On Being Brought from Africa to America," in *Poems on Various Subjects, Religious and Moral*, 17 (Denver, CO: W.H. Lawrence & Co., 1887), 17.

50   Regina Jennings, "African Sun Imagery in the Poetry of Phillis Wheatley," *Pennsylvania English* 22:1-2 (2000): 68-72. In fact, Wheatley's contemporary and first African-American published poet, Jupiter Hammon, criticized Wheatley's frequent usage of what he considered to be "heathen" images in her poetry. This critique ironically came in the context of an ode praising Wheatley, Jupiter Hammon, "An Address to Miss Phillis Wheatley, Ethiopian Poetess, in Boston, Who Came from Africa at Eight Years of Age, and Soon Became Acquainted with the Gospel of Jesus Christ," in *The Collected Works of Jupiter Hammon: Poems and Essays*, ed. Cedrick May, 11-13, (Knoxville, TN: University of Tennessee Press, 2017), 11.

51 Phillis Wheatley, "To the Right Honourable William, Earl of Dartmouth, His Majesty's Principal Secretary of State for North America," in *Poems on Various Subjects, Religious and Moral*, 66-68 (Denver, CO: W.H. Lawrence & Co., 1887), 67.

52 Olaudah Equiano, *The Interesting Narrative of the Life of Olaudah Equiano* (New York, NY: Penguin Books, 1995), 3-4.

53 Equiano, *Interesting Narrative*, 20.

54 Equiano, *Interesting Narrative*, 189-190.

55 Equiano, *Interesting Narrative*, 191.

56 Ignatius Sancho, *Letters of the Late Ignatius Sancho, An African* (New York, NY: Penguin Books, 1998), 92.

57 Equiano, *Interesting Narrative*, 77.

58 Equiano, *Interesting Narrative*, 233.

59 Ottobah Cugoano, *Thoughts and Sentiments on the Evil and Wicked Traffic of the Slavery and Commerce of the Human Species* (Cambridge: Cambridge University Press, 2013), 146.

60 Cugoano, *Thoughts and Sentiments*, 30.

61 Ottobah Cugoano, *Thoughts and Sentiments*, 13-14.

62 Frederick Douglass, *Narrative of the Life of Frederick Douglass: An American Slave* (Cambridge, MA: Belknap Press, 2009), 115.

63 Harriet Jacobs, *Incidents in the Life of a Slave Girl* (Mineola, NY: Dover Publications, 2001), 60.

64 Jacobs, *Incidents*, 63-64.

65 Jacobs, *Incidents*, 65.

66 Booker T. Washington, *Up From Slavery: An Autobiography* (New York, NY: Doubleday, Page & Co., 1901), 16.

67 Marcus Garvey, "Should A Foreign Foe Invade?" in *The Marcus Garvey and Universal Negro Improvement Association Papers*, ed. Robert A. Hill (Berkeley, CA: The University of California, 1990), 224.

68 Malcolm X, *The Autobiography of Malcolm X* (New York, NY: Random House, 1964), 424.

69 *Autobiography of Malcolm X*, 277.

70 Bengt Sundkler, *Bantu Prophets in South Africa* (Cambridge: Lutterworth Press, 1948), 13.

71 Taken from the King James Version; other modern translations stick more closely to the Hebrew name "Cush."

72 Reggie L. Williams, *Bonhoeffer's Black Jesus: Harlem Renaissance Theology and an Ethic of Resistance* (Waco, TX: Baylor University Press, 2014), 25.

73 Howard Thurman, "Love," in *African-American Religious Thought: An Anthology*, eds. Cornel West & Eddie S. Glaude, Jr.49-61 (Louisville, KY: Westminster John Knox Press, 2003), 55.

74 Howard Thurman, *Jesus and the Disinherited*, (New York, NY: Abingdon-Cokesbury Press, 1949), 32.

75 Thurman, *Jesus and the Disinherited*, 28.

76 Raphael G. Warnock, *The Divided Mind of the Black Church: Theology, Piety, and Public Witness* (New York, NY: New York University Press, 2014), 3.

77 Susanne Scholz, "Stirring Up Vital Energies: Feminist Biblical Studies in North America (1980s- 2000s)," in *Feminist Biblical Studies in the Twentieth Century: Scholarship and Movement*, ed. Elizabeth Fiorenza Schüssler (Atlanta, GA: Society of Biblical Literature, 2014), 53-70.

78 Derek Kidner, *Genesis* (Downers Grove, IL: InterVarsity Press, 2019), 209.

79 David L. Stubbs, *Numbers* (Grand Rapids, MI: Brazos Press, 2009) 208; Timothy Ashley, *The Book of Numbers* (Grand Rapids, MI: Eerdmans Publishing, 1993), 543.

80 Louis Ndekha, "The Daughters of Zelophehad and African Women's Rights: A Malawian Perspective on the Book of Numbers 27:1-11," *AJGR* 19 no. 2 (2013). 37-51.

81 Wilda Gafney, *Womanist Midrash: A Reintroduction to the Women of the Torah and the Throne* (Louisville: Westminster John Knox Press, 2017), 161.

82 Elizabeth C. Stanton, *The Woman's Bible* Part 1 (New York, NY: European Publishing, 1895); Susanne Scholz, *Introducing the Women's Hebrew Bible: Feminism, Gender Justice, and the Study of the Old Testament* (London: Bloomsbury T&T, 2017); Phyllis Trible, *Texts of Terror: Literary-Feministic Readings of Biblical Narratives* (Philadelphia, PA: Fortress Press, 1984); Esther Fuchs, *Sexual Politics in the Biblical Narrative: Reading the Hebrew Bible as a Woman* (New York, NY: Sheffield Academic Press, 2000); Elizabeth Schüssler Fiorenza, *Wisdom Ways: Introducing Feminist Biblical Interpretation* (Maryknoll, NY: Orbis Book, 2001).

83 Fiorenza, *Wisdom Ways*, 9.

84 Helen Schüngel-Straumann, "Genesis 1-11 The Primordial History," in *Feminist Biblical Interpretation: A Compendium of Critical Commentary on the Books of the Bible and Related Literature*, eds. Luise Schottroff and Marie-Theres Wacker, 1-14 (Grand Rapids: William B. Eerdmans, 2012).

85 Alice Walker, *In Search of Our Mothers' Gardens: Womanist Prose* (New York, NY: Harcourt, 1983); Audre Lorde, *Sister Outsider: Essays and Speeches* (Berkeley, CA: The Crossing Press, 1984); Maya Angelou, *The Heart of a Woman* (New York, NY: Random House, 1981); Renita Weems, *Just a Sister Away* (Philadelphia, PA: Innisfree Press, 1988); Katie Cannon, *Katie's Canon: Womanism and the Soul of the Black Community* (New York, NY: Continuum, 1995); Jacquelyn Grant, *White Women's Christ and Black Women's Jesus* (New York, NY: Oxford University Press, 1989), Delores Williams, *Sisters in the Wilderness: The Challenge of Womanist God-Talk* (Maryknoll, NY: Orbis Books, 1993); Juliana Claassens, "Give us a Portion Among our Father's Brothers': The Daughters

of Zelophehad, Land, and the Quest for Human Dignity," *JSOT* 37 (2013): 319-37.

86 Nyasha Junior, *An Introduction to Womanist Biblical Interpretation* (Louisville, KY: Westminster JohnKnox Press, 2015), 59; Gay Byron and Vanessa Lovelace, *Womanist Interpretations of the Bible: Expanding the Discourse* (Atlanta, GA: SBL Press, 2016).

87 Mitzi J. Smith, *I Found God in Me: A Womanist Biblical Hermeneutics Reader* (Eugene, OR: Cascade Books, 2015).

88 Williams, *Sisters*, 7.

89 Raymond F. Surburg, "The Presuppositions of the Historical-Grammatical Method as Employed by Historic Lutheranism," *The Springfielder* 38 no. 4 (1974): 278-88.

90 Kidner, *Genesis*, 138; Kenneth Mathews, *Genesis* (Nashville, TN: B&H Publishing, 2005), 174.

91 Gafney, *Womanist Midrash*, 5.

92 Katharine Sakenfeld, "Zelophehad's Daughters," *PRSt* 15 (1988): 37-47.

93 Sakenfeld, "Zelophehad's Daugthers," 40.

94 Katharine Sakenfeld, "In the Wilderness, Awaiting the Land: The Daughters of Zelophehad and Feminist Interpretation," *PSB* 9 (1988): 179-86.

95 Sakenfeld, "In the Wilderness," 194-195.

96 Sakenfeld, "Zelophehad's Daughters," 37.

97 Claassens, "Give us a Portion," 337.

98 Claassens, "Give us a Portion," 334.

99 Claassens "Give us a Portion," 321.

100 Yael Shemesh, "A Gender Perspective on the Daughters of Zelophehad: Bible, Talmudic Midrash, and Modern Feminist Midrash," *BibInt* 15 (2007): 80-109.

101 Shemesh, "A Gender Perspective," 83-84.

102 Shemesh, "A Gender Perspective," 97.

103 Gafney, *Womanist Midrash*, 162.

104 Gafney, *Womanist Midrash*, 163.

105 Gafney, *Womanist Midrash*, 159-160.

106 R. Dennis Cole, *Numbers* (Nashville, B&H Publishing, 2000), 460.

107 Cole, *Numbers*, 460-461.

108 Cole, *Numbers*, 460-461.

109 Cole, *Numbers*, 541.

110 Cole, *Numbers*, 460.

111 Cole, *Numbers*, 460.

112 Raymond Brown, *The Message of Numbers: Journey to the Promised Land* (Downers Grove, IL: InterVarsity Press, 2002), 244-45.

113 Sakenfeld, "Zelophehad's Daughters," 40.

114 Brown, *The Message of Numbers*, 244.

115 Brown, *The Message of Numbers*, 306.

116 Stubbs, *Numbers*, 207.

117 Stubbs, *Numbers*, 208.

118 Stubbs, *Numbers*, 210.

119 Glen Martin and Max Anders, *Holman Old Testament Commentary* (Nashville, TN: Broadman & Holman Publishers, 2002), 374.

120 Douglas Stuart, *Word Biblical Commentary: Hosea-Jonah*, vol. 31 (Grand Rapids, MI: Zondervan, 1988), 297.

121 Cleotha Robertson, "Amos," in *The Africana Bible: Reading Israel's Scriptures from Africa and the African Diaspora*, ed. Hugh R. Page, Jr. (Minneapolis, MN: Fortress Press, 2010), 174.

122 Gary V. Smith, "Continuity and Discontinuity in Amos' Use of Tradition," in *The Journal of the Evangelical Theological Society* 34.1 (1991), https://www.etsjets.org/files/JETS-PDFs/34/34-1/34-1-pp033-042_JETS.pdf

123 Unless otherwise noted, all biblical citations in this chapter are taken from the New International Version.

124 Stuart, *Hosea-Jonah*, 321.

125 Francis Brown and S.R. Driver, *The Brown-Driver-Briggs Hebrew and English Lexicon: With an Appendix Containing the Aramaic Coded with the Numbering System from Strong's Exhaustive Concordance of the Bible* (Peabody, MA: Hendrickson Publishers, 1996), 1033.

126 Stuart, *Hosea-Jonah*, 321.

127 One can see the idea of divine sovereignty in the list of oracles that is initially addressed to surrounding foreign nations and then to Judah, the Southern Kingdom, and to Israel, the Northern Kingdom, in Amos 1 and 2.

128 The Plagues against Egypt are to be seen as warfare between Yahweh and the gods of Egypt. Each plague represents a different deity of the Egyptian pantheon. With the Exodus, all of the gods are defeated by Yahweh.

129 There are authors who have addressed the issue of war imagery as a means of revelation by Yahweh. An exceptional one that addresses this in both the Old and New Testaments is Tremper Longman III & Daniel G. Reid, *God is a Warrior* (Grand Rapids, MI: Zondervan Publishing, 1995).

130 Stuart, Hosea-Jonah, 373; Jeffrey Niehaus, "Amos," in *The Minor Prophets: An Exegetical and Expository Commentary*, ed. Thomas Edward McComiskey (Grand Rapids, MI: Baker Books, 1992), 456.

131 Stuart calls this list "a reference list of covenant curses," *Hosea-Jonah,* xxxiv. The list shows the continuity of the book of Amos

with that of the Pentateuch. Moreover, this connection exhibits the idea that Stuart develops regarding the nature of prophets and prophecy. He claims that prophets are not original but, on the contrary, they are quotations and re-contextualizations of the curses and blessings in the Pentateuch.

132 Stuart, *Hosea-Jonah*, 373.

133 Gary V. Smith, *The NIV Application Commentary: Hosea, Amos, Micah* (Grand Rapids, MI: Zondervan Publishing, 2001), 350.

134 David Allan Hubbard, *Tyndale Old Testament Commentaries: Joel and Amos* (Downers Grove, IL: InterVarsity Press, 1990), 234.

135 Cf. Am. 1:1; the definite article attached to the word for earthquake exhibits that Amos has a particular earthquake in mind that would be readily known to the readers.

136 Hubbard, *Joel and Amos*, 235.

137 Stuart, *Hosea-Jonah*, xxxix.

138 Stuart, *Hosea-Jonah*, 393.

139 The line of argument is that if I relocated the Nubians, I surely relocated you.

140 Brown and Driver, *Hebrew Lexicon*, 748.

141 The use of Exodus language again points to the historicity of the Exodus from the vantage point of Amos. This point the writer will develop later.

142 The opening oracles that are addressed exhibit the sovereignty of the Lord in that He holds accountable to covenant violations and violations against humanity, both His chosen people and the surrounding nations.

143 Gary H. Hall, "*shamad*" in *New International Dictionary of Old Testament Theology and Exegesis,* vol. 4 (Grand Rapids, MI: Zondervan Academic, 2012), 152.

144 Hall, "*shamad*," 152.

145 Stuart, *Hosea-Jonah*, 349.

146 Duane A. Garrett, *A Commentary on Exodus* (Grand Rapids, MI: Kregel Publications, 2014), 469.

147 Howard Thurman, *Jesus and the Disinherited* (Boston: Beacon Press, 1996), 12.

148 Dennis R. Edwards, "Good Citizenship: A Study of Philippians 1:27 and its Implications for Contemporary Urban Ministry," *Ex Auditu* 29 (2013), 74-93.

149 Lynn H. Cohick, "Philippians and Empire: Paul's Engagement with Imperialism and the Imperial Cult," in *Jesus Is Lord, Caesar Is Not: Evaluating Empire in New Testament Studies*, ed. Scot McKnight and Joseph B. Modica (Downers Grove: IVP Academic, 2013), 166.

150 Ibid., 175.

151 See Cohick, "Philippians and Empire," 166.

152 Miroslav Volf, "Soft Difference: Theological Reflections on the Relation Between Church and Culture in 1 Peter," *Ex Auditu* 10 (1994), 16.

153 Barth L. Campbell, *Honor, Shame, and the Rhetoric of 1 Peter*, 1st edition (Atlanta: Scholars Press, 1998), 112.

154 See John H. Elliott, "Disgraced Yet Graced: The Gospel According to 1 Peter in the Key of Honor and Shame," *BTB* 25 (1995), 166-78.

155 Mary Beard, *SPQR: A History of Ancient Rome*, 1st Edition (New York: Liveright, 2015), 521.

156 Campbell, *Honor, Shame*, 12.

157 John H. Elliott, *1 Peter: A New Translation with Introduction and Commentary*, First Edition AB (New York: Anchor Bible, 2001), 117.

158 See Dennis R. Edwards, *Might from the Margins: The Gospel's Power to Turn the Tables on Injustice* (Harrisonburg: Herald Press, 2020).

159 Steven Richard Bechtler, *Following in His Steps: Suffering, Community, and Christology in 1 Peter* (Society of Biblical Literature, 1998), 81.

160 Elliott argues at length for this view in both his commentary (*1 Peter*, 476-83) and throughout his sociological study (*Home for the Homeless*), as well as in other writings.

161 "The issue is the suffering of believers treated as social-cultural strangers and aliens. The encouragement that our author [Peter] offers is not that the addressees are pilgrims on their way to a heavenly home, but that they have already been granted a home in the household of God" (Elliott, *1 Peter*, 483). It is unlikely that Peter uses the specialized vocabulary of *parepidēmos* and *paroikia* in a metaphorical way to suggest that his audience is alienated from their heavenly homeland. Such an idea is found in Heb 11:13-16 using similar vocabulary but with a different point to make than Peter. See Paul J. Achtemeier, *Peter 1* Hermeneia (Minneapolis: Fortress Press, 1996), 175.

162 Bechtler, *Following in His Steps*, 143.

163 Karen H. Jobes, *1 Peter* (Grand Rapids: Baker Academic, 2005), 169.

164 Fordham University. http://www.fordham.edu/halsall/source/pliny1.asp

165 Stephen C. Barton, "Social Setting of Early Non-Pauline Christianity" in *Dictionary of the Later New Testament & Its Developments* (Edited by Ralph P. Martin and Peter H. Davids. Downers Grove: IVP Academic, 1997), 1108.

166 Jobes, *1 Peter*, 187. See Bechtler, *Following in His Steps*, 167.

167 Achtemeier, *Peter 1*, 190.

168 The more common word, *doulos*, occurs in 2:16 and is used metaphorically for all Christians in service to God. Achtemeier, *1 Peter*, 194, alleges that even though the word *oiketai* refers to household slaves, "it can also be used generically for slaves and is

probably to be understood in that way here [1 Pet 2:18]."

169 J. Ramsey Michaels, *1 Peter*, Volume 49 (Grand Rapids: Zondervan, 2015), 138.

170 Volf, "Soft Difference," 22.

171 Ibid., 23.

172 Beard, *SPQR*, 304.

173 Many commentators discuss the status of women in Ancient Rome. See Achtemeier, *1 Peter*, 206-07 and especially David Balch, *Let Wives Be Submissive: The Domestic Code in 1 Peter* (Chico, CA: Society of Biblical Literature, 1981).

174 Green, *1 Peter*, 212

175 Ibid., 212.

176 Ephrem the Syrian, *Madrashe on Faith*, ed. Jeffrey T. Wickes (Washington, DC: The Catholic University of America Press, 2015), 156.

177 Edward G. Mathews, Jr. & Joseph P. Amar, *The Fathers of the Church: St. Ephrem the Syrian: Selected Prose Works* (Washington, DC: The Catholic University of America, 1994), 13.

178 Peter Brown, *Poverty and Leadership in the Later Roman Empire* (Hanover, NH: University Press of New England, 2002), 19.

179 Eusebius of Caesarea, *Life of Constantine*, ed. Averil Cameron & Stuart G. Hall (Oxford: Clarendon Press, 1999), 1:5.

180 Peter Brown, *The Rise of Western Christendom: Triumph and Diversity, A.D. 200-1000*, 10th ed. (Malden, MA: Wiley-Blackwell, 2013), 61.

181 Gregory of Nazianzus, *On the Love of the Poor and Those Afflicted with Leprosy*, ed. M.F. Toal, in *The Sunday Sermons of the Great Fathers 4: From the Eleventh Sunday after Pentecost to the Twenty-Fourth and Last Sunday after Pentecost* (San Francisco, CA: Ignatius Press, 2000), 56.

182 Gregory of Nazianzus, *On the Love of the Poor*, 58.

183   Steven J. Friesen, "Injustice of God's Will? Early Christian Explanations of Poverty" in *Wealth and Poverty in Early Church and Society*, ed. Susan R. Holman, 17-36 (Grand Rapids, MI: Baker Academic, 2008), 21.

184   Bruce L. Shelley, *Church History in Plain Language*, 3rd ed. (Nashville, TN: Thomas Nelson, 2008), 124.

185   Shelley, *Church History*, 124.

186   H.H. Pope Shenouda III, *The Nature of Christ* (Cairo: Dar El-Tebaa El-Kawmia, 1997), 9.

187   Timothy Aelurus, *Against Chalcedon*, ed. R.Y. Ebied and L.R. Wickham, in *After Chalcedon: Studies in Theology and Church History Offered to Professor Albert van Roey*, ed. and trans. C. Laga, J.A. Munitiz, and L. Van Rompay, 115-166 (Leuven: Peeters, 1985), 141.

188   Maged Mikhail, *On Cana of Galilee: A Sermon by the Coptic Patriarch Benjamin I* in *CCR* 23.3, 66-93 (2002), 81.

189   Ironically, even black liberation theologians—while critiquing the "dehumanization" inherent in Western Christendom and its creedal attempts at framing orthodoxy—yet deploy a Eurocentric method of centralizing Roman and European sources in their theological discourse and maintaining councils such as Chalcedon as "defining moments," see Eboni Marshall Turman, *Toward a Womanist Ethic of Incarnation: Black Bodies, the Black Church, and the Council of Chalcedon* (New York, NY: Palgrave Macmillan, 2013), 38.

190   For examples of Western scholarly expressions of racism with regard to early African theology, see E.L. Woodward, *Christianity and Nationalism in the Later Roman Empire* (London: Longmans, Green, 1916), who attributes the triumph of Christianity in Upper Egypt to the "backwardness" of the Egyptian people, p. 11.

191   Walter Bauer, *Orthodoxy and Heresy in Earliest Christianity* (Philadelphia, PA: Fortress Press, 1971), 287. On the influence of Bauer on patristic studies, see Paul A. Hartog, *Orthodoxy and*

Heresy in Early Christian Contexts: Reconsidering the Bauer Thesis (Eugene, OR: Wipf and Stock, 2015).

192 Soong-Chan Rah, *The Next Evangelicalism: Freeing the Church from Western Cultural Captivity* (Downers Grove, IL: InterVarsity Press, 2009), 30.

193 Jeffrey T. Wickes, *St. Ephrem the Syrian: The Hymns on Faith* (Washington, DC: The Catholic University of America Press, 2015), 23.

194 David O. Moberg, *The Great Reversal: Reconciling Evangelism and Social Concern*, 2nd ed. (Eugene, OR: Wipf and Stock, 2006), 13.

195 James E. Goehring, *Ascetics, Society, and the Desert: Studies in Early Egyptian Monasticism* (Harrisburg, PA: Trinity Press International, 1999), 17.

196 David Brakke and Andrew Crislip, *Selected Discourses of Shenoute the Great: Community, Theology, and Social Conflict in Late Antique Egypt* (Cambridge: Cambridge University Press, 2015), 17.

197 Shenoute of Atripe, *Not Because a Fox Barks*, ed. David Brakke and Andrew Crislip in *Selected Discourses of Shenoute the Great: Community, Theology, and Social Conflict in Late Antique Egypt*, 201-205 (Cambridge: Cambridge University Press, 2015), 203.

198 Shenoute, *Not Because a Fox Barks*, 204-205. Shenoute quotes here from Rom. 2:8-9.

199 Much of Black liberation theology sees the Christian claim of universal truth as an extension of Western Enlightenment hegemony, David Tracy, "African-American Thought: The Discovery of Fragments," in *Black Faith and Public Talk: Critical Essays on James Cone's Black Theology and Black Power*, ed. Dwight N. Hopkins, 29-38 (Waco, TX: Baylor University Press, 2007), 37.

200 Cone, *Black Theology and Black Power*, 120; Cone here argues that "the experience of oppression itself" is the "ultimate authority" in framing orthodox belief.

201 Richard Allen, *The Life, Experience, and Gospel Labours of the Rt. Rev. Richard Allen* (Philadelphia, PA: F. Ford and M.A. Riply, 1880), 13.

202 Allen, *Life, Experience, and Gospel Labours*, 13.

203 C. Eric Lincoln and Lawrence H. Mamiya, *The Black Church in the African American Experience* (Durham, NC: Duke University Press, 1990), vii.

204 See Gen. 3, especially v. 12. Unless otherwise noted, all biblical citations are from the NIV.

205 This also aligns with the African concept of *ubuntu*, defined by the saying, "A person is a person through other persons." It is also a rebuke of Western romantic ideals of individualism.

206 Henri Tajfel and John C. Turner, "The Social Identity Theory of Intergroup Behavior," in *Psychology of Intergroup Relations*, eds. S. Worchel, W. G. Austin, 7-24 (Chicago, IL: Nelson-Hall Publishers, 1986).

207 J. Kameron Carter, *Race: A Theological Account*, (Oxford: Oxford University Press, 2008), 229.

208 Carter, *Race: A Theological Account*, 229.

209 Willie James Jennings, *The Christian Imagination: Theology and the Origins of Race* (New Haven, CT: Yale University Press, 2010), 58, 113-114.

210 Allen, *Life, Experience, and Gospel Labours*, 12.

211 Anne H. Pinn and Anthony B. Pinn, *Fortress Introduction to Black Church History* (Minneapolis: Augsburg Fortress, 2002), 28-29.

212 Lincoln and Mamiya, *Black Church*, 51. They cite an edited version of Allen's account (ed. George A. Singleton (New York,

NY: Abingdon, 1960), 24-25) which claims that the mutual aid society was formed "without regard to religious tenets," but I have not found this wording in other versions.

213 Allen, *Life, Experience, and Gospel Labours*, 13.

214 Allen, *Life, Experience, and Gospel Labours*, 13.

215 Allen, *Life, Experience, and Gospel Labours*, 12.

216 See Richard S. Newman, *Freedom's Prophet: Bishop Richard Allen, the AME Church and the Black Founding Fathers* (New York, NY: NYU Press, 2008); Charles Wesley, *Richard Allen: Apostle of Freedom* (Washington, DC: Associated Publishers, 1935); Carol George, *Segregated Sabbaths: Richard Allen and the Rise of Independent Black Churches, 1760-1840* (New York, NY: Oxford University Press, 1973).

217 Allen, *Life, Experience, and Gospel Labours*, 12.

218 Allen, *Life, Experience, and Gospel Labours*, 14-15.

219 Pinn and Pinn, *Fortress Introduction to Black Church History*, 31.

220 Pinn and Pinn, *Fortress Introduction to Black Church History*, 28.

221 John Dixon Long, *Pictures of Slavery in Church and State* (New York, NY: Negro Universities Press, 1969), 27-28, cited in Pinn and Pinn, *Fortress Introduction to Black Church History*, 29.

222 Pinn and Pinn, *Fortress Introduction to Black Church History*, 29-30.

223 Newman, *Freedom's Prophet*, 48.

224 Cynthia Lynn Lyerly, *Methodism and the Southern Mind, 1770-1810* (New York, NY: Oxford University Press, 1998), 58.

225 Manning Marable and Leith Mullings, *Let Nobody Turn Us Around: Voices of Resistance, Reform, and Renewal: An African American Anthology*, 2nd ed. (Lanham, MD: Rowman & Littlefield, 2000), 19.

226 Allen, *Life, Experience, and Gospel Labours*, 11.

227 Allen, *Life, Experience, and Gospel Labours*, 18.

228 George, *Segregated Sabbaths*, 77; Pinn and Pinn, *Fortress Introduction to Black Church History*, 33.

229 Charles Spurgeon, *The Power in Praising God* (New Kensington, PA: Whitaker House, 1998), 148.

230 Tajfel and Turner, "The Social Identity Theory," 8.

231 Eph. 2:11-18.

232 Yehudith Auerbach, "The Reconciliation Pyramid—A Narrative-Based Framework for Analyzing Identity Conflicts," *Political Psychology*, 30.2, 291-318 (April 2009): 310. See also Zheng Wang, "Old Wounds, New Narratives: Joint History Textbook Writing and Peacebuilding in East Asia," *History and Memory*, 21.1 (2009): 101-126, and Herbert C. Kelman, "Conflict Resolution and Reconciliation: A Social-Psychological Perspective on Ending Violent Conflict Between Identity Groups," in *Landscapes of Violence: An Interdisciplinary Journal Devoted to the Study of Violence, Conflict and Trauma* 1.5, 1-9 (2010): 6. Available at: http://scholarworks.umass.edu/lov/vol1/iss1/5.

233 Eph. 2:13.

234 1 Cor. 2:13.

235 1 Cor. 12:21-26.

236 1 Cor. 12:19-24, from *The Message* translation.

237 1 Cor. 12:18, 24 respectively.

238 Col. 1:18.

239 1 Cor. 12:26, *The Message*.

240 Allen, *Life, Experience, and Gospel Labours*, 12.

241 Allen, *Life, Experience, and Gospel Labours*, 18 (emphasis mine).

242 Vincent Bacote, "Gifts from 'Father Abraham,'" *Comment* (Aug. 1, 2005), 12-13.

243 Kuyper makes the following statement while entertaining the question about the contribution of Calvinism to human development (quoted at length for context): "The fact that in a given circle Calvinism has formed an interpretation of life quite its own, from which both in the spiritual and secular domain a special system arose for domestic and social life, justifies its claim to assert itself as an independent formation. But it does not yet credit it with the honor of having led humanity, as such, up to a higher stage in its development, and therefore this life-system has not, so far as we have yet considered it, attained that position which alone could give it the right to claim for itself the energy and devotion of our hearts. In China it can be asserted with equal right that Confucianism has produced a form of its own for life in a given circle, and with the Mongolian race that form of life rests upon a theory of its own. But what has China done for humanity in general, and for the steady development of our race? Even so far as the waters of its life were clear, they formed nothing but an isolated lake. Almost the same remark applies to the high development which was once the boast of India and to the state of things in Mexico and Peru in the days of Montezuma and the Incas. In all these regions the people attained a high degree of development, but stopped there, and, remaining isolated, in no way proved a benefit to humanity at large. *This applies more strongly still to the life of the colored races on the coast and in the interior of Africa—a far lower form of existence, reminding us not even of a lake but rather of pools and marshes,*" Abraham Kuyper, *Lectures on Calvinism* (Grand Rapids, MI: Eerdmans, 1931), 32. (italics mine)

244 Kuyper, *Lectures*, 35.

245 Kuyper, *Lectures*, 196.

246 I say "theological-ethical" because I resist the common bifurcation of theology and ethics. Christian beliefs are not merely matters of confession; God desires a people who believe Him and behave in a manner that emerges from our reception/understanding

of His revelation to us. Such a unity of belief and action is characteristic of the Black Christian tradition, which we here call Gospel Haymanot.

247 Daniel José Camacho, "Common Grace and Race," *Reformed Journal*, January 10, 2015. https://reformedjournal.com/common-grace-and-race/. Camacho sees Kuyper's doctrine of common grace tied to views of racial hierarchy, though here he also concludes that Kuyper can still be helpful. In my view, the connection he makes is plausible in theory but not accurate, though he rightly asks how we must account for Kuyper's views on race in connection to his theological claims.

248 e.g., Kuyper's language of common grace.

249 Kuyper himself saw his approach to Calvinism as working with and refining the tradition rather than simply passing it on.

250 Though he may have thought he was making descriptive statements that were obvious to an average nineteenth-century observer, they betray a disdain for those who are not European and perhaps for those particularly from Africa.

251 Figures such Jonathan Edwards, George Whitefield, James Henley Thornwell, and Robert Lewis Dabney are prime examples.

252 McQueen on his use of long takes in *12 Years a Slave*: "As far as the long take was used in this film, for example, during the beating of Patsey, that is particularly one take because I wanted it in real time. I wanted the tension to build. It's like a circle. It just goes faster, spins faster, faster, and faster like a whirling dervish spinning to get close to God, in some ways. The eye of the storm is Michael Fassbender whipping, first counterclockwise and then clockwise. This is very technical what I'm talking about. What's going on there emotionally is devastating. What has to match that is the choreography of the camera and the action. I didn't want to put a cut in there because, once you put a cut in there, you let the audience off the hook. It's almost like they're allowed to breathe," Steve McQueen, "Director's Cut: Steve McQueen (12 Years a Slave),"

interview by Calum Marsh, *MTV.com,* October 16, 2013, http://www.mtv.com/news/2771146/12-years-a-slave-steve-mcqueen-interview/.

253 Likewise, the Ethiopic word *haymanot* means "belief," "theology" and "faith"—of which God is the principal object.

254 While close attention to certain figures may not precipitate crises at the level I describe, sustained attention to the life and work of any figure will reveal their human frailty, and it is important to develop a strategy for contending with the clay feet of those we study.

255 James D. Bratt, *Abraham Kuyper: Modern Calvinist, Christian Democrat* (Grand Rapids: Wm. B. Eerdmans Publishing Co., 2013).

256 Vincent Bacote, "Vincent Bacote: 'Critical thinking is obeying the commandment of loving your neighbor as yourself,'" interviewed by Bart Noort, accessed February 12, 2020, https://stevebishop.blogspot.com/2014/10/kuyperania-october-2014.html

257 Gospel Haymanot keeps these two loves together, whereas they are sometimes separated amid the bifurcation of theology and ethics characteristic of modern post-Enlightenment theology (conservative or liberal).

258 It is because of my encounter with quotes such as these that I became a critical thinker instead of a zero- sum thinker. This critical thinking disposition is vital in our engagement with all figures and ideas.

259 I will use the terms "Black People," "African-Americans" and "The People" interchangeably. Using the term "The People" returns a humanizing quality so long and often extracted from the general cultural references to African-Americans in the U.S. and resists the negative cultural connotations of anything modified with the descriptor word 'Black.' Doing so is also an homage to the ways in which some Native American nations refer to themselves within their own languages as 'person' or 'people.' For instance, the Dine'e (pronounced 'di-nay'), which is a term meaning 'People' and has been used to reference the Navaho and Abachi Nations within their own cultures (http://www.native-languages.org/apache). This

referencing also raises the specter of the First Nations' traumatic histories when encroaching Europeans stole the majority of their lands, now called the United States, frequently engaging in genocidal actions.

260   John N. Briere and Catherine Scott, *Principles of Trauma Therapy: A Guide to Symptoms, Evaluation, and Treatment (DSM-5 Update)*, 2nd ed. (Thousand Oaks, CA: Sage Publications, 2015).

261   Nathaniel V. Mohatt, "Historical Trauma as Public Narrative: A Conceptual Review of How History Impacts Present-Day Health," in *Social Science & Medicine* 106 (April 2014): 128-136, http://dx.doi.org/10.1016/j.socscimed.2014.01.043; Shulamith Lala Ashenberg Straussner and Alexandrea Josephine Calnan, "Trauma through the Life Cycle: A Review of Current Literature," in *Clinical Social Work* 42 (2014): 323- 335.

262   Sandra L. Bloom, "Every Time History Repeats Itself, the Price Goes Up: The Social Reenactment of Trauma," in *Sexual Addiction & Compulsivity* 3.3 (1996): 161-194, https://doi.org/10.1080/10720169608400111; Graham Danzer, "White Psychologists and African Americans' Historical Trauma: Implications for Practice," in *Journal of Aggression, Maltreatment & Trauma* 25 (2016): 351-370, https://doi.org/10.1080/10926771.2016.1153550.

263   ALANA is an acronym for African American, LatinX, Asian, and Native American.

264   Phia S. Salter, Glenn Adams, and Michael J. Perez, "Racism in the Structure of Everyday Worlds: A Cultural-Psychological Perspective," in *Current Directions in Psychological Science* 27.3, 150-155 (June 2018), 151. http://doi.org/10.1177/0963721417724239.

265   J. Kameron Carter, *Race: A Theological Account*, (New York, NY: Oxford University Press, 2008), 229-230.

266 Salter, Adams and Perez, "Racism," 151; Shawn O. Utsey, Joseph G. Ponterotto, and Jerlym S. Porter, "Prejudice and Racism, Year 2008--Still Going Strong: Research on Reducing Prejudice With Recommended Methodological Advances," in *Journal of Counseling and Development*, 86 (3), 339-347 (2008): 339, 342; Shawn O. Utsey, "Cultural, Sociofamilial, And Psychological Resources That Inhibit Psychological Distress in African Americans Exposed to Stressful Life Events and Race-Related Stress," in *Journal of Counseling Psychology* 55.1, 49-62 (2008): 50, 58, https://www.researchgate.net/publication/224071411_Cultural_Sociofamilial_and_Psychological_Resources_That_Inhibit_Psychological_Distress_in_African_Americans_Exposed_to_Stressful_Life_Events_and_Race-Related_Stress

267 Jonathan Kanter, "A Preliminary Report on the Relationship Between Microaggressions Against Black People and Racism Among White College Students," in *Race and Social Problems* 9.4, 291–99 (2017): 291, 292, 294, 296, https://doi.org/10.1007/s12552-017-9214-0.

268 Thema Bryant-Davis and Carlota Ocampo, "The Trauma of Racism: Implications for Counseling, Research, and Education," in *The Counseling Psychologist* 33, 574-578 (2005): 574-575.

269 William E. Cross, Jr., "Black Psychological Functioning and the Legacy of Slavery: Myths and Realities. " in *International Handbook of Multigenerational Legacies of Trauma*, ed. Y. Danieli, 387-400, (New York, NY: Plenum Press, 1998), 389.

270 Cross, "Black Psychological Functioning," 389.

271 Jacquelyn Grant, *White Women's Christ and Black Women's Jesus: Feminist Christology and Womanist Response* (Atlanta, GA: American Academy of Religion, 1989), 10-11.

272 Carter, *Race*, 378-379.

273 Emmett G. Price, "There is a Balm in Gilead: A Call to Lament Together," in *A Time for Sorrow: Recovering the Practice of Lament in the Life of the Church*, eds. Scott Harrower and Sean

M. McDonough, 89-100 (Peabody, MA: Hendrickson Publishers, 2019), 92.

274 Negro Spiritual, modern arrangement by Richard Smallwood, "I Love the Lord," No. A3 in *Give Us Peace: Richard Smallwood & Union Temple Young Adult Choir*, Gerald Lewis Recording: August 25, 1976, vinyl.

275 Sam Cooke, "A Change Is Gonna Come," No. B1 in *Ain't That Good News*, RCA Victor: February 18, 1964, vinyl.

276 Price, "Balm in Gilead," 99-100.

277 Rom. 8:26-27, unless otherwise noted, all biblical citations in this chapter are from the NIV.

278 Ps. 42:5.

279 Ps. 42:1-2, 6-8.

280 Heather Davediuk Gingrich and Fred C. Gingrich, *Treating Trauma in Christian Counseling* (Downers Grove, Illinois: InterVarsity Press, 2017), 23.

281 Is. 55:8-11.

282 Is. 18:2,7; Song 1:5.

283 Num. 12:10; while some have argued that Miriam and Aaron challenged Moses' authority based on his marriage to a foreigner—with no specific issue with a Cushite—it has also been persuasively argued that Miriam and Aaron harbored specific animosity towards this Cushite woman because there was no mention of any issue with Moses having married Zipporah, a Midianite foreigner. Also, the divine punishment of a skin affliction is an irony that cannot be incidental, given how Cushite skin evoked the fascination and exoticization of the ancient world, Rodney Steven Sadler Jr., *Can a Cushite Change His Skin? An Examination of Race, Ethnicity, and Othering in the Hebrew Bible* (New York, NY: T&T Clark, 2005), 39.

284 Phillis Wheatley, "An Hymn to Humanity," in *Poems on Various Subjects*, 61.

285 J. Deotis Roberts, *Black Theology in Dialogue* (Philadelphia, PA: The Westminster Press, 1987), 24.

286 Roberts, *Black Theology*, 25.

287 Roberts, *Black Theology*, 27.

288 Jacobs, *Incidents*, 65

289 Acts 1:8.

290 Is. 58:6.

291 Jas. 2:17.

292 Acts 5:29.

293 Acts 4:19-20.

294 Acts 5:28.

295 Acts 5:17.

296 Virgilio Elizondo, *Galilean Journey: The Mexican-American Promise* (Maryknoll, NY: Orbis Books, 1983), 87.

297 Gen. 18:18; Mt. 25:31-46.

298 Rom. 1:18-32; 2 Jn. 2:18-27.

299 Acts 4:12.

300 Roberts, *Liberation and Reconciliation*, 8.

301 Acts 5:33-39.

302 Mt. 28:16-20.

303 Ex. 8:1.

www.ingramcontent.com/pod-product-compliance
Lightning Source LLC
Chambersburg PA
CBHW021058080526
44587CB00010B/286